Spare Time Guides, No. 7

SPARE TIME GUIDES SERIES
Ann J. Harwell, Editor

SPARE TIME GUIDES:
Information Sources for Hobbies and Recreation, No. 7

Weaving, Spinning, and Dyeing

LAVONNE BRADY AXFORD

1975
Libraries Unlimited, Inc.
Littleton, Colorado

LIBRARIES UNLIMITED, INC.
P.O. Box 263
Littleton, Colorado 80120

Library of Congress Cataloging in Publication Data

Axford, Lavonne B
    Weaving, spinning, and dyeing.

    (Spare time guides ; no. 7)
    Bibliography: p.
    Includes index.
    1. Textile crafts--Bibliography. 2. Textile crafts
--Equipment and supplies--Directories. 3. Publishers
and publishing--Directories. I. Title.
Z6153.T4A94   [TT699]   016.7461   75-16436
ISBN 0-87287-080-4

PREFACE

The Spare Time Guides series was conceived to provide librarians with selective, annotated lists of recommended books on specific hobbies and recreational activities, and also to help craftsmen and do-it-yourselfers learn more about their hobbies and crafts.

Because of the current interest in leisure time activities—and the resultant increase in the number of books concerning these activities—it has become difficult for librarians and hobbyists to determine just which books will fit their specific needs. Few selection aids on hobbies are available: the reviewing media that serve librarians devote little space to books on crafts and leisure time activities, and a search of hobby and crafts magazines reveals relatively few book reviews. In too many cases, the main source of information on crafts books is the promotional material provided by the publishers, which does not usually offer a critical evaluation of the work. The Spare Time Guides series is designed to provide sufficient information to enable librarians and hobbyists to distinguish between books of varying quality.

Although there has always been a small band of craftsmen dedicated to perpetuating the ancient skills of weaving, spinning, and dyeing, the ranks of such craftsmen have recently been swelled. During the 1960s and early 1970s, many people found these basic natural crafts to be an attractive means of offsetting the sterility and impersonality of urban life. The increasing popularity of the fiber crafts has resulted in the appearance of numerous how-to-do-it books at all levels of experience. Such books vary greatly not only as to the level of their intended audience but also as to the competence of their execution, and it is not always easy to determine just which book will best serve one's needs—or the needs of one's patrons.

Lavonne Brady Axford, a professional librarian who is also a skilled weaver, has examined all kinds of publications on the fiber crafts—from four-page pamphlets to four-color picture books. She gives complete bibliographic information for each entry (including pagination and price), and her thorough annotations describe the strengths and weaknesses of the works. Chronologically, coverage extends through 1974.

The main sections of the bibliography, divided by subject, list and annotate 389 books. These cover not only the main topics of the bibliography—i.e., weaving, spinning, dyeing (including batik and tie-dye)—but also such related crafts as basket weaving, bobbin lace, sprang, color and design as related to fiber crafts, macramé, and rug hooking. Following these subject-arranged sections is the periodicals section, which provides bibliographic information and annotations for 25 periodicals in the field. There is a directory of organizations and supply houses and a directory of publishers; this last is particularly important because many of the publishers in the field are relatively obscure.

Those who need to sift through the multitude of books on the fiber crafts will find substantial assistance in this seventh volume of the Spare Time Guides series.

Ann J. Harwell
Editor, Spare Time Guides

TABLE OF CONTENTS

INTRODUCTION

The subjects covered in this bibliography are handweaving (which also includes general books on textiles), dyeing and resist dyeing (batik and tie-dye), spinning, and related crafts (baskets, bobbin lace and sprang, macramé, rug hooking). Also included are books on color and design as they relate to the crafts covered. Because these subjects are often interrelated in the craft books themselves, they can be logically grouped together for this bibliography. Books are entered under the headings listed above; however, periodicals for all subjects are treated in a single alphabet.

Craft books, like cook books, are so personal to the user that it is necessary to study each title quite closely to see if it will fit one's needs. Because participants range from those with a short-lived craft interest to serious craftspersons to artists, there is a need for a correspondingly wide range of titles. For example, does *Beyond Craft* stimulate or repel? Is *Great Tapestries* history plus inspiration for the future, or is it only history—and dusty at that? Readers of these books will include craftsmen, hobbyists, professionals in sundry textile fields, artists, and historians; it is a happy combination of crafts that can offer wide and deep interest to so many.

The beginning or introductory books listed here will generally be useful for older children as well as for adults. No "play books" have been included, since the crafts are too intricate for that approach. A few of the more serious craft books for children have been listed. However, since the small child cannot attempt any of these crafts without supervision, the books chosen for inclusion in these categories are mainly those aimed at the adult who is teaching the young child. The older child can read and follow the simple craft books as well as an adult can. Encyclopedia-type sources have been excluded from this bibliography.

Just as a craftsman's age is of no importance to his success as a craftsman, the age of a craft book is not relevant to its usefulness. In addition, the method of production (mimeograph, slick, or anything between) cannot serve as an indication of value. Finally, the usual sources of in-print books (*Books in Print* or *Paperback Books in Print*) do not necessarily lead to craft books, since many are privately printed. These privately printed books should not in any way be confused with vanity press publications; they present essential information that is unavailable elsewhere. Many craftsmen do not want to make the effort necessary for commercial publication, and they choose to make their knowledge available in less formal ways.

Craft titles appear and disappear with a bewildering suddenness. The best place to find information on new books, supplies, and other craft needs is always the craft magazine; this bibliography includes some of the more important titles.

Most craftsmen are friendly people who are willing to share their information. A letter of inquiry to Noël Bennet about her teaching schedule elicited a warm, personal, handwritten response, as did one to Paula Simmons on fleeces. An airmail request to the *Quarterly Journal of the Guilds of Weavers, Spinners and Dyers*, on the availability of fleeces for spinners in Great Britain produced a handwritten airmail response: fleeces are seldom available from the growers in Great Britain because each grower is allowed to keep only four for his own use; the rest go to the Wool Board. Fleeces are available for export from the Wool Board. Choose the type you want and then inquire. It is possible, however, to obtain some types of English fleece from Straw into Gold (see the list of suppliers, page 126).

Lists of periodicals, craft organizations, and publishers have been included, as well as a list of sources of supplies, materials, and equipment. The titles in the bibliography itself are organized into the categories listed and described below. Because this approach is inherently and unavoidably arbitrary, it is absolutely necessary that the user consult the index in order to be sure of locating all the titles on a given subject.

HANDWEAVING

Studying the age-old art of weaving makes one aware of the common bonds of the past and the present and the continuity of the human experience. The loom, the spindle, and the spinning wheel represent a timeless technology that links the modern craftsman to his ancient ancestors in a particularly personal way. Even one experience with this form of communion creates an insatiable yearning for more.

An important note to readers of weaving books: expert weavers know and beginners should be forewarned that one must always work out one's own draft fully on paper, including counting threads, before beginning to prepare the warp. Among the titles reviewed for this book there was scarcely one that did not have typographical errors, drafting errors, or errors in the instructions. Therefore, the weaver would be well advised to consult more than one source before starting a project, whether it be a weaving project or the construction of a loom or other type of weaving equipment. Books are seldom 100 percent correct on all details, as they are written and published by fallible human beings. Errata sheets are not much help; often they do not get into the first few copies printed, or they may get lost. So keep your own records and ask other weavers about errors they might have found in the books they have consulted.

On the other side of the coin, no matter how detailed and technical it is, weaving is fun. One of Shakespeare's characters in *Henry IV*, Part I, muses, "If I were a weaver, I could sing all manner of songs." So, start weaving and sing a little!

SPINNING

The history of every culture and every age comes alive to those who take up spinning. The newcomer to spinning wool, for instance, discovers a new world. The spinner, as a rule, is not satisfied with using factory produced rolags. He wants to choose his fleece, then sort, pick, wash, card, and dye it, and then proceed with the spinning. Each step in the process can be directed precisely toward achieving the effect wanted for the finished product, be it a rug or a baby blanket. Truly dedicated spinners usually own their own sheep. Most of us are less fortunate, but we at least learn the types of sheep and the kind of wool each produces, how they are fed, and something about shearing and its importance to the spinner. We also visit the local farms and take in the spring lamb shows. In addition, one also buys fleece from abroad and becomes acquainted with the growers, spinners, and suppliers in other countries.

Spinning of cotton and flax also leads one to research ancient techniques and methods, to correspond with spinners at home and abroad, and to develop interests never before contemplated. For camel and other animal hairs and wool (except dog), the average person must be satisfied with buying it by the pound. However, I suspect that there has been more than one avid spinner who has haunted the local zoo when the camels and llamas are moulting and who has obtained (by gift or by nefarious means) a pound or two of hair. John Dyer in his poem "The Fleece," written in 1757, said, "A different spinning every different web asks from your glowing fingers." The art of spinning could scarcely be better described.

DYEING AND RESIST DYEING

Chaucer's prologue to the *Canterbury Tales* speaks of a "webbe," a "dyere," and a "tapicier" among the pilgrims wending their way to the shrine of St. Thomas à Becket. Indeed, one can hardly imagine a world without the magic of dye stuffs and the wealth of visual delight that they make possible. Craftsmen use both natural and chemical dyes to obtain exactly the color they want. The end product is more predictable when chemical dyes are used; however, a great many people find natural dyeing to be particularly fascinating. Each leaf, flower, or other natural dye stuff differs in color depending on its freshness, the time of the year, etc. Consequently, each dye bath is an experiment. Books and charts can at the most only guide the beginner as he undertakes this exciting search. Because there are too many details to trust to memory, those devoted to natural dyeing keep meticulous records, for future reference, of each batch of dye they produce. There are definite advantages to planting your own dye garden. For instance, it can free you of the necessity of lurking around the gardens and yards of other people, coveting plants that might produce exciting colors. Since natural dyeing can become a passion, it is fortunate that most enthusiasts are dedicated environmentalists who avoid harvesting plants in such quantities as to prohibit propagation (e.g., lichen) or taking bark from trees not already dead.

However popular natural dyeing might be now, it is seldom that the dyer actually gets back to the basics as described in the following passage from the *Penny Encyclopedia for the Diffusion of Useful Knowledge*, published during the 1830s and 1840s: "The bath must be replenished with dung from time to time, as it gets exhausted by the passage of mordanted goods." However, the author personally knows of some devotees who use urine as a mordant.

The resist dye techniques for creating colored cloth became popular in the elementary and high schools of the United States (often to the detriment of the crafts themselves). However, many of the books now available on both tie-dye and batik restore them to their former level of art form.

RELATED CRAFTS AND OTHER ASPECTS

BASKETS

One of man's oldest crafts, but also new as a bright penny, basket making remains always a fascinating art. Some of the new books on the subject, such as Rossbach's, bring basketry into the last quarter of the twentieth century alive and doing well.

BOBBIN LACE AND SPRANG

Bobbin lace and sprang have reappeared on the scene suddenly and quite dramatically as major crafts. Of course, having such an internationally known weaver as Peter Collingwood write on sprang has given it quite a boost. Watching the growing interest in these techniques gives one a miniaturized view of the entire craft revival.

COLOR AND DESIGN

Color and design books (and particularly design) are numerous. One can only hope to find a few that lift the spirit and stimulate the imagination. The end result, however, can often be worth the search; like everyone, craftsmen need to grow and change. The books presented here are a sample of those available.

MACRAMÉ

Macramé, the technique of knotting, has infinite variety and possibilities. Projects can be huge, tiny, bristly, brilliant with color, or monochrome. Macramé can use sailors' knots, Victorian or ultra-modern patterns and techniques, or free-form design. It can be used alone or combined with other techniques. Weavers often use macramé to advantage in finishing hangings or other pieces. Macramé is constantly experiencing popular revivals; one wonders whether it ever actually passes from the scene.

RUG HOOKING

Hooking, particularly rugs, is an old craft that has remained popular through time. The new surge of interest is not only for plain rug hooking but also for shuttle hooking, egg beater hooking, and latch hooking. The latch hook is probably the most popular technique at the present time; it is not only easy to learn, but also readily available in kit form.

Lavonne Brady Axford

HANDWEAVING

FLOOR LOOMS (PLANS)

1. Mathieson, David. **Building the Oregon Loom: Detailed Instructions for Making a Loom at Home Using Handtools and Easily Obtained Materials.** Eugene, Ore., Serenity Weavers, 1973. n.p. illus. $4.50pa.

   This is a beautifully produced book on building a four-harness, counterbalanced, 45-inch, weaving-width floor loom. Every aspect of the construction is covered.

2. Payton, Curtis C. **The Aloha Loom, Plans and Specifications.** McMinnville, Ore., Robin and Russ Handweavers, 1973. 17p. illus. $5.50pa.

   Contains photographs, detailed drawings, and clear plans for a 24-inch, 30-inch, 36-inch, and 45-inch counterbalanced loom, including a sectional warp beam.

3. Reed, Tom. **Loom Book.** Santa Fe, N.M., Sunstone, 1973. 63p. illus. $5.95.

Mr. Reed has provided instructions and illustrations on how to build a 40-inch, four-harness, counterbalanced loom. He also tells how to get the needed materials. However, one would surely want to see many different loom plans (see subject index) and talk to experienced weavers before deciding which loom to build—or whether to build one at all.

4. Worst, Edward F. **How to Build a Loom**. Pacific Grove, Calif., Select Books, 1973; repr. from 1918 ed. 19p. illus. $2.50pa.

This is Chapter 11 from Worst's *Foot Power Loom Weaving*. Here are complete working drawings for a 18-inch Danish and a 47-inch Swedish counterbalanced, four-harness loom with hanging beaters and six-foot pedals, including accessories and a fly shuttle beater. Recently reprinted, it is a classic in the field. The handweaver who wants to build his own loom would do well to look at this work as well as at other titles on building looms (see the subject index).

HANDWEAVING ON FLOOR LOOMS
(Two-Harness to Multiharness)

5. Albers, Anni. **On Weaving**. Middletown, Conn., Wesleyan University Press, 1974; repr. of 1965 ed. 204p. illus. $17.50; $6.95pa.

An excellent presentation of textile fundamentals and the underlying principles of weaving. The book includes an early history of textiles by the author, who contributed the article on handweaving in the 1963 edition of the *Encyclopaedia Britannica*. This is an excellent source book for weavers and for those who are interested in the art of weaving rather than in how-to-do-it books. Znamierowski (entry 115), Regensteiner (entry 58), and many others have listed this book as a basic title in their bibliographies.

6. Allard, Mary. **Rug Making: Techniques and Design**. New York, Chilton, 1963. 160p. illus. $7.50.

This book, which deals with the age-old craft of rug weaving and design, fully explores the techniques used in weaving pile rugs (knotted, looped, floated, or hooked). In addition, the author covers the techniques for weaving flat or non-pile rugs such as double weaving, soumak, or tapestry. The importance of shape in rug design is investigated. The book is listed in Regensteiner (entry 58), and other important bibliographies. The author, who is a teacher and designer, has a good background in weaving and has produced a work that is valuable for providing an overview of the many facets of rug weaving and design. Her step-by-step instructions are adequate. If one were seriously interested in weaving a Navajo rug or a tapestry, however, a book dealing specifically with the technique would be far more useful—for instance, Noël Bennett's *Working with the Wool* (entry 119) or Mary Pendleton's *Navajo and Hopi Weaving* (entry 126) for Navajo rugs and Beutlich's *Technique of Woven Tapestry* (entry 173). The book is indexed.

7. Allen, Helen Louise. **American and European Handweaving.** Rev. Madison, Wisc., R. K. Harris, n.d.; limited ed. rev. from Madison, Wisc., Democratic Weaving Co., 1939. 94p. illus. $6.00pa.

This work was based on the author's teaching notes. Ms. Allen worked the notes into a fine introduction for the handweaver or someone interested in reading about weaving, but it is not a how-to-do-it book. She speaks of surface plain weave, added threads, open work, four-harness weaving, tapestry, weaving in India, patterns, looms, and other subjects. Bibliography. Regensteiner (entry 58) lists her in her bibliography, as do other weavers.

8. Atwater, Mary Meigs. **Byways in Handweaving.** New York, Macmillan, 1954. 128p. illus. $7.95.

Another title by the "dean of American Handweavers," well done as always. It deals with small or non-loom weaves such as card, tablet, inkle and plaiting, Maori twining, and belt weaves. Most of them are from other countries—for instance, Egypt, Peru, Mexico, and Guatemala. She has included a chapter on the uses of handicraft in occupational therapy. The beginner will use this book easily and the experienced weaver will want it also. After reading this, the multiharness weaver will want to try card or inkle weaving. Mrs. Atwater confines herself to very traditional patterns. One would have to go to Candace Crockett's *Card Weaving* (entry 137) and some of the other new titles to get anything with a contemporary look.

9. Atwater, Mary Meigs. **Recipe Book: Patterns for Handweavers.** Rev. from the 1st ed. Published by the Mary M. Atwater Weavers Guild; distr. Salt Lake City, Wheelwright Lithography Co., 1957. 140p. illus. $8.00pa.

Weaving shops such as Robin and Russ have this important book by one of the great teachers and weavers. The guild put out the revision as a unique contribution to the advancement of the art of weaving. Ms. Atwater considered this book to be her most useful. The directions assume that one knows how to weave and read drafts. Four-harness to ten-harness weaves are given for such items as coverlets, rugs, drapery and upholstery, fabrics for clothing, table pieces, towelling, bags, and blankets.

10. Atwater, Mary Meigs. **The Shuttle-Craft Book of American Hand Weaving.** Rev. ed. New York, Macmillan, 1951. 341p. illus. $8.95.

Subtitle: "being the account of the rise, development, eclipse, and modern revival of a national popular art. Together with information of interest and value to collectors, technical notes for the use of weavers, and a large collection of historic patterns." Even this lengthy description, however, does not fully preview the contents. This work, considered a "bible" by everyone in the field, was written by the "dean of American handweavers." Of particular interest are the historical sketches preceding the description of each type of weave (such as overshot, twill, and summer and winter). Many of the 132 illustrations and almost 300 patterns are for four-harness looms, although some are for multiharness. The whole book is well done.

11. Beck, Dorothy, and Hazel Chase. **Weaver's Answer Book.** Distr. Hingham, Mass., Bare Cove Weavers, 1962. 106p. illus. $4.50pa.

A plain, straightforward, practical book for the beginner weaver who is working alone. It answers such questions as what type of loom to buy, what accessory equipment is needed, how many reeds are needed, etc. Basic instructions and simple projects are given. It also includes loom plans and drawings of accessory pieces that can be made in the home workshop.

12. Black, Mary E. **New Key to Weaving.** Milwaukee, Wisc., Bruce Publishing Co., 1961. 571p. illus. $12.00.

Excellent chapters on looms, loom parts, warping, and dressing make this book basic to any collection. As with Atwater (entry 10) and others, this book is for the beginner in four-harness weaving, but it is also one that the more experienced weaver can also delve into as a reference work, as a browsing book, or for an expansion of his ideas. Each draft is accompanied by a photograph of the finished product plus complete directions for weaving, tie-up, and treadling order. Twill and twill derivatives receive a lot of attention, as do tartans and the Gobelin tapestry technique. A special section listing weaving terms in foreign languages is helpful. A chapter devoted to the theory of weaving will enable the weaver to develop designs of his own. This book is known as one of the "bibles" in the field.

13. Black, Mary E. **The Sett and Weaving of Tartans.** Shelby, N.C., Lily Mills Co., n.d. 47p. illus. $2.00pa.

Fifteen full-color plates of tartans help guide the weaver. The directions are clear, as one would expect from the author. Everything is here: a brief history, an explanation of the weaving, and how to beat properly to get the desired effect. It is primarily for the four-harness loom and, of course, for the experienced weaver. This discussion is much more detailed than the chapter on tartans in Black's *New Key to Weaving* (entry 12). For other books on tartans, see the annotation for Christian Hesketh's *Tartans* (entry 201).

14. Blum, Grace D. **Functional Overshot.** West Chicago, Ill., Grace D. Blum, 1960. 27p. illus. $16.50pa.

Thirty-two lovely swatches of functional overshot weaves are included in Ms. Blum's porfolio. Complete instructions are given for draft, color key, and objectives of the weave, and there are also ideas for use and a discussion of problems to watch for. These are basic sources for modern and historic fabric design. All were created by and for the four-harness loom. The weaver's need for swatches, not photographs or diagrams, is well met here. Beautifully woven and quite fine (at 30 ends per inch), the patterns are well presented. Although the beginner has a definite need to see actual pieces of patterns, the intermediate and expert weaver have the same need. A weaver can always use new and different sources of inspiration.

15. Blumenau, Lili. **The Art and Craft of Handweaving: Including Fabric Design.** New York, Crown, 1968. 136p. illus. $3.95.

An introduction to handweaving that includes fabric design, yarns, looms and tools, weave and structure, forms of design, and the actual procedure of weaving. The narrative is supplemented by 192 photographs and drawings. Regensteiner (entry 58) and others list Blumenau as a basic text.

16. Blumenau, Lili. **Creative Design in Wall Hangings.** New York, Crown, 1967. 213p. illus. $7.95.

The author, a lecturer and instructor in the fabric design department of the Philadelphia College of Art, has done a superlative job in this book, which she subtitles "weaving patterns based on primitive and medieval art." A history of wall hangings, past and present, constitutes part of the book. The beginner should be able to create a wall hanging from the instructions, and should also feel at home in the craft. The more experienced weaver can also gain from the book, since the illustrations, mostly photographs, are particularly well done. Often the modern hangings pictured are works of famous artists. Indexed.

17. Brown, Harriet J. **Handweaving for Pleasure and Profit.** New York, Harper, 1952. 273p. illus. $5.95.

A guide to harness weaving for beginners (especially those who work by themselves) and for more advanced weavers who are seeking new ideas or help on a fundamental problem. The author has written and illustrated this guide with exceptional clarity. She has reduced the most complicated techniques to simple, step-by-step instructions that are easily followed. An excellent bibliography and glossary are included as well as an index. It would be difficult to praise this book too highly; it is probably the most definitive work on two-harness weaving. As an added feature, it contains a discussion of teaching the blind to weave.

18. Burnham, Harold B., and Dorothy K. Burnham. **Keep Me Warm One Night: Early Handweaving in Eastern Canada.** Published in cooperation with the Royal Ontario Museum by the University of Toronto Press, 1972. 387p. illus. $27.50.

A wealth of information is contained in this beautiful book. It is an excellent, comprehensive historical survey (to 1900) of Canadian handweaving, with an emphasis on settlement influence and the problems of production. This study is the result of 25 years of work by the textile department of the Royal Ontario Museum. It covers spinning and weaving tools and equipment for clothing, blankets, rugs, and linens. However, the heaviest emphasis is on coverlets. Over 500 line drawings and photographs (including drafts) supplement the narrative. Experienced but non-professional weavers will be able to use this book; they will find here 8- and 10-harness overshot drafts that are not easily available in the usual weaving book. Good bibliography. By all means, see this book.

19. Chetwynd, Hilary. **Simple Weaving.** New York, Watson-Guptill, 1969. 104p. illus. $2.50.

"Small but very informative," says Jean Wilson of Mr. Chetwynd's book. It covers looms, weaving accessories, yarns for weaving, designing the warp, dressing the loom, weaving problems, drafts, finishing, and more, all shown in both color and black and white. Bibliography.

20. Collingwood, Peter. **The Techniques of Rug Weaving.** New York, Watson-Guptill, 1969. 513p. illus. $17.50.

If possible, buy it! To say that Collingwood, one of England's leading weavers, has written the most complete book on rug weaving and finishing is an understatement. Beginning weavers and experts alike will find ideas here for rugs and innumerable other projects—pillows, hangings, etc. In fact, every weaver will want at least to look at this work. The book includes many of Collingwood's original answers to problems that needed solving. The illustrations are remarkably clear and most of the photographs are of the author's own works. A bibliography and index add to the book.

21. Cook, Bonny. **Weaving with (Second Hand) Fur.** Bainbridge Island, Wash., Bonny Cook, 1972. 27p. illus. $3.50pa.

The author presents a unique approach to weaving. This is a complete how-to-do-it book for creating items from old furs: how, why, and what to weave from discarded fur coats and fur collars, and how to choose the fur. Projects are illustrated with good photographs, both color and black and white. The flea market and second-hand clothes stores await; here, indeed, is your opportunity to do your own thing. The book is fun to browse through even if you aren't ready for a project using old fur. The ideas could lead to a new approach for any weaver.

22. Creager, Clara. **Weaving: A Creative Approach for Beginners.** New York, Doubleday, 1974. 192p. illus. $3.95pa.

Clara Creager, who teaches weaving at Ohio State University, has written and illustrated (black and white) a guide to contemporary weaving techniques on and off a loom. She deals with looms, yarns, dressing the loom, weaving processes and tricks of the trade, basic weaves and drafting, loom or harness controlled weaves, basic variations in plain weave and surface techniques. The techniques are clearly illustrated and would be easy to follow. There is also a glossary and a supply source list.

23. Cyrus, Ulla. **Manual of Swedish Handweaving**. Tr. by Viola Anderson. Newton Centre, Mass., Branford, 1956. 250p. illus. $5.95.

Although it is now out of print, this manual is included here because it probably will be back in print shortly. A "bible" in the handweaving field, it is listed in virtually every bibliography on hand weaving. It was translated from a best-selling Swedish text. There are clear instructions, with hundreds of illustrations, for handweaving on a loom using Swedish as well as universal techniques. The section on types of looms is excellent. In addition, there is a Swedish-English word list.

24. Davenport, Elsie G. **Your Handweaving**. Pacific Grove, Calif., Craft and Hobby, 1970; repr. of 1948 ed. 128p. illus. $4.25pa.

This book on the frame loom and the four-harness loom emphasizes practical craftsmanship. The book was written particularly for those who have little or no opportunity to have personal instruction. The author clearly and concisely explains not only all weaving techniques, but also the rationale for these techniques. The illustrations supplement the narrative well. Elsie Davenport has written major texts on dyeing and hand spinning; this one on weaving upholds her reputation as a first-rate author in the craft field.

25. Davison, Marguerite Porter. **A Handweaver's Pattern Book**. Rev. ed. Swarthmore, Pa., Marguerite P. Davison, 1950. 217p. illus. $10.00.

A book that every weaver needs, and a "bible" of the craft. Although the 345 threading directions are all for the four-harness loom, an experienced weaver will get lots of ideas for patterns on looms with more harnesses. There are photographs of each pattern and complete instructions, although this is not really a how-to-do-it book. For each threading, several variations, with threadling and tie-ups, are shown so that the weaver can see the difference. Weavers, from beginners through experts, will want to have this book. An excellent bibliography is included, as well as an index.

26. Davison, Marguerite Porter. **A Handweaver's Source Book**. Swarthmore, Pa., Marguerite P. Davison, 1953. 240p. illus. $12.00.

Beautifully printed in sepia, this is a treasury of drafts for the weaver of four-harness overshot. The author selected the drafts from the Laura M. Allen Collection, which was made early in the century when some of the famous nineteenth century weavers were still alive. The drawings of the patterns are almost full-page size, and they truly show the pattern. Full directions are included. Everyone will want this book; it is a wonderful view of history, but totally modern in application. There are two pages of photos of the original written drafts, and the drafts include the name of the weaver from whom the weave was obtained.

27. Davison, Marguerite P. **Pennsylvania-German Home Weaving**. Swarthmore, Pa., Marguerite P. Davison, 1947. illus. $1.00pa.

This was originally Volume Four of the "Home Craft Course" by Mrs. C. Naoman Keyser, Plymouth Meeting, Pa. (1947). "After two printings, this book is rewritten, giving instructions of the source material, with directions for reproducing many of the weavings." Many of the simple techniques used in early textiles have been forgotten. The Pennsylvania-German area has many of these textiles made by master craftsmen, and the textiles can be very instructive to modern weavers. They also complete the picture of the period; these views of authentic textiles add to our ideas of the furnishings of this style.

28. Estes, Josephine. **Miniature Patterns for Handweavers**. Newton, Mass., Josephine Estes, 1956. 2 parts. illus. $5.00pa.

The author has prepared drafts for miniature pattern weaving, with 24 different miniatures in each part. These are overshot patterns reduced so they may be used on book marks or as borders for place mats, towels, etc. The first part includes Chariot Wheel, Lovers Knot, Star of Bethlehem, etc. The second part has Maltese Cross, Young Lovers Knot, Church Windows, and others. Many guilds have used these interesting and well done patterns as projects. Gertrude Greer's *Adventures in Weaving* (Peoria, Ill., Manual Arts Press, 1951) also has miniatures such as Whig Rose, Weaver's Fancy, etc. It is a book worth looking for, although it is out of print at the present time.

29. Farrow, Hazel. **Painted Warp**. Los Altos, Calif., Handweavers, 1974; also distr. by Nilus Leclerc. 42p. illus. $4.00pa.

Everything you need to know about painting a warp in preparation for weaving. The book was written by an expert, and the illustrations are delightfully humorous.

30. Folts, Teressa, and David Mathieson. **Warping the Loom Alone**. Eugene, Ore., Serenity Weavers, 1972. 42p. illus. $4.95pa.

This is a beautiful, meticulously produced book on warping a floor loom alone. The black and white drawings of each step are lovely. It is aimed at beginning weavers who are teaching themselves or whose instructor has not been sufficiently clear. However, there may well be more experienced weavers, dissatisfied with their warping method, who will pick up some pointers.

31. Francisco, Irene. **Opening a Door to Two Harness Techniques.** Shelby, N.C., Lily Mills Co., 1960. 52p. illus. $2.00pa.

Very well done and exceptionally clear, this pamphlet is aimed at the handweaver who is already familiar with the names of the parts of the loom, weaving terms in general, and the fundamentals of plain tabby weaving. Each section has a photograph of the finished product as well as diagrams. The first section includes lace techniques (leno, Spanish lace, and Danish medallion); the second handles simple inlay; the third, Monk's Belt technique; and the fourth, Dukagang. The instructions are broken down into steps that no one could fail to understand.

32. Frey, Berta. **Four Harness Weaving.** West Hartford, Conn., HGA Scholarship Fund/Berta Frey, 1972. 18p. $1.50pa.

This is a transcription of a New England Weavers' Seminar lecture in 1971 by Berta Frey, who is admired and loved by handweavers. Ms. Frey has something for every level of weaver. Although a how-to-do-it section is included, the pamphlet should be read primarily for stimulation. The proceeds from the sale of this pamphlet go to the Handweavers' Guild of America Scholarship Fund.

33. Frey, Berta. **Seven Projects in Rose Path.** McMinnville, Ore., Robin and Russ Handweavers, 1972; repr. of 1948 ed. published by the author. 29p. illus. $3.00pa.

The projects were originally planned and written for a Weavers' Guild program. Since the program was conducted by correspondence, the instructions, draw downs, etc., were mimeographed. After the seven projects were completed, they were collected into this pamphlet. Although weavers taking the course represented varying degrees of experience, it was assumed that they could weave and read drafts. The pamphlet is geared to the four-harness loom, although there is quite a bit also on eight harnesses. It is highly recommended.

34. Gallagher, Constance Dann. **Linen Heirlooms: The Story of a Collection of the 19th Century Handwoven Pieces with Directions for Their Reproduction.** Newton Center, Mass., Branford, 1968. 209p. illus. $13.00.

The author located the pieces to study and drew by hand the drafts and designs. This is a truly scholarly effort. Almost all of the pieces studied have now been placed permanently in the Division of Textiles, Smithsonian Institution. A history of each towel, pillow case, etc., is given, plus a draft that the weaver of today could easily follow. Also included is a history of the weaving equipment, patterns used in the 1800s, suggestions for the reproduction of early linens, and a section on the care of fine linen. Altogether an interesting and unusual book.

35. Garrett, Cay. **Warping All by Yourself.** Santa Rosa, Calif., Threshold, 1974. 160p. illus. $2.95pa.

A clear, well illustrated book (180 illustrations) by Cay Garrett of the Yarn Depot, who has for years successfully taught beginning and experienced weavers to use this method of warping the loom by oneself.

36. Grierson, Ronald. **Woven Rugs.** 2nd ed. Leicester, England, Dryad Press, 1960. 60p. illus. $1.95pa.

A detailed discussion, with excellent diagrams, of the handweaving of rugs, from tapestry to knotted pile. One chapter deals with the loom, its parts, and how it works. Further chapters explain traditional tapestry techniques for rugs, contemporary weaving design, and color. Mr. Grierson is well known in the field and is listed in such bibliographies as Regensteiner (entry 58).

37. Groff, Russell E. **Sectional Warping Made Easy.** McMinnville, Ore., Robin and Russ Handweavers, n.d. 25p. illus. $2.50pa.

For those handloom weavers with four or more harnesses and a sectional warp beam that they don't know how to use, here is the book on sectional warping. Complete directions include both concise text and excellent photographs. Directions are also included for dressing the loom after the warp is on the sectional warp beam. Weavers who think they are not interested in using this method might like to browse through Mr. Groff's book anyway, since many weavers turn to this method when putting on a long warp or a difficult yarn.

38. Hall, Eliza C. **A Book of Handwoven Coverlets.** Rutland, Vt., Charles E. Tuttle Co., 1970; first published in 1912. 411p. illus. $8.75.

The author tells the story behind such handwoven designs as Lovers Knot, Youth and Beauty, and Rose in the Wilderness. The book is obviously designed for those interested in early American weaving. The plates are good; there are instructions for creating coverlets, but they could be used only as a starting point, not as complete drafts.

39. Harvey, Virginia I. **Bateman Weaves.**

This is not a full entry, but simply a "good news item." Ms. Harvey will publish William Bateman's manuscript, with notes and clarification, in about three years (1977). All handweavers will await this book with interest, but particularly the multiharness weaver.

40. Hayes, Marie C. **Swedish-English Weaving Glossary.** Distr. in U.S., Avon, Conn., Book Barn, 1973. 24p. $3.95pa.

A dictionary of double-columned pages with Swedish to English translations of weaving terms. Reference collections and weavers with access to materials in the Swedish language will want it. Because of the amount of excellent but untranslated Swedish material for weavers, this book is a must. In addition to the translations of terms and numbers, there are also conversion tables for inches, feet, yards, and reed sizes.

41. Held, Shirley E. **Weaving: A Handbook for Fiber Craftsmen.** New York, Holt, Rinehart and Winston, 1973. 372p. illus. $13.95; $9.95pa.

A balanced, well-written (and equally well-illustrated) complete handbook for the beginner that will also be helpful for the experienced weaver. The chapter headings tell the story: the origins of fabric; the evolution of the non-loom processes; handweaving of the past; the first six millenia; handweaving of the past: Europe, the Far East, and the New World; twentieth century handweaving; materials for weaving; tools and equipment; preparation for weaving; drafting; loom-controlled weaves; weaver-controlled weaves; finishing procedures; pile weaves; simple looms; non-loom techniques; hand spinning; yarn dyeing; yarn printing; elements and principles of design; designing for the loom; contemporary fiber craftsmen; appendices (drafts for four-harness loom, records, sources of materials and supplies, yarn designations, and metric conversion tables); and finally, bibliography, notes, glossary, and index. Highly recommended as a first purchase for libraries and individual weavers.

42. Ickis, Marguerite. **Weaving as a Hobby.** New York, Sterling, 1968. 72p. illus. $3.95.

This nicely done book is meant for the beginning or prospective weaver. The text, well illustrated, covers the home-made frame loom as well as two-harness and four-harness looms. The author explains how to dress the looms and has step-by-step projects for each type of loom.

43. Kirby, Mary. **Designing on the Loom.** London, Studio, 1955; repr. Pacific Grove, Calif., Select Books, 1973. 96p. illus. $6.25pa.

Ms. Kirby, assuming that the reader can weave and probably read drafts, opens up the world of fabric designing on the loom. The chapters cover planning a fabric; reading instructions; plain weave; color and weave effects; tweed, woolen, and worsted dress fabrics; keeping records; weaves for looms up to four-harness; weaves for looms between five- and eight-harnesses; using a loom with two warp beams; weaves and designs for sixteen-harness looms; and designing for Jacquard woven fabrics. A necessary book for most weavers and, of course, particularly for the fabric weaver.

44. Kroncke, Grete. **Mounting Handicraft.** New York, Van Nostrand Reinhold, 1973. 96p. illus. $4.50.

The techniques of finishing and mounting are beautifully and carefully presented in this book from the Scandinavian Craft Series. If a piece of weaving needs to be transformed into a bag, lampshade, book cover, or other article, here is the book with explicit directions and diagrams. Although it is obviously aimed at the weaver who is already producing, the beginner will find ideas galore.

45. Lourie, Janice R. **Textile Graphics: Computer Aided.** New York, Fairchild, 1973. 279p. illus. $15.00.

A technical, well-done book that will be of interest to specific libraries and individuals. Ms. Lourie has combined the Jacquard loom with an IBM 5/360 and IBM 2250. She covers weaving fundamentals and then explains the loom/computer design principles. For those able to handle it, the information is fascinating and perfectly logical.

46. Millen, Rogers. **Weave Your Own Tweeds.** Swarthmore, Pa., Marguerite P. Davison, 1948. 31p. illus. $4.00pa.

The author, a well-known weaver of tweeds, recognizes the problems of tweed weaving and gives full directions on how to avoid them. It is a unique book in the field. All aspects of equipment, characteristics of yarn, warping, tying on, process of weaving, selvage, patterns and color are thoroughly discussed, with clear directions and illustrations. Supplementary patterns are found in *Handweaver's Pattern Book* (entry 25). Any weaver, at any level, interested in tweeds needs this book. It also includes a working drawing for a counterbalanced, rigid loom with an overhead beater.

47. **Monsterblad (patterns).** Stockholm, Förlag, 1953-63. Folder. $2.50 to $5.50 depending on issue.

Fifteen volumes were published; most are out of print, but some still turn up occasionally and a weaving bibliography would be incomplete without mentioning them. Each consists of a pamphlet giving tie-ups, reed spacing, etc., for Swedish handwoven patterns, plus color plates of the woven patterns. All are in Swedish but some have an added section of English translation.

Rugs, tablecloths, and bed coverings were shown. These important examples of the weaver's art have been basic to the weaver's library for years.

48. Moorman, Theo. **Weaving as an Art Form**. New York, Van Nostrand Reinhold (announced for Spring 1975). 96p. illus. $9.95.

At last, a book by Theo Moorman describing the "Moorman technique" and its uses. The author, a famous English artist, designer, and weaver, writes of her training, gives sources of information for the weaver, and includes a chapter on commissioned works (which discusses both the opportunities and the problems).

49. **Helps and Hints**. Hartford, Conn., Handweavers Guild of America, (announced for Spring 1975). price not set.

This booklet has been compiled from successful projects used by weaver volunteers in rehabilitation centers, demonstration projects, nursing homes, etc. It will be of great help to others involved in this kind of work.

50. Newman, Margaret, and Bertha Needham. Pamphlets. Clearwater, Fla., M. Newman, 1960– . $1.00 each postpaid.

Between them, these two well-known weavers have prepared the following leaflets, all of which contain information that is well worth the price:

Four Harness Mats (Needham): 10 interesting mats, including rose mat in "Silver Stars" with swivel instructions; Turned Spot Bronson; geometric swivel design on coarse linen ground, M's and O's in texture effect; bath mat with pastel warp on "Whig Rose" with diamond border; and others.

Honeysuckle Anthology (Needham): seven pages, containing 236 variations of Honeysuckle. Besides the many borders and all-over figures, there is a page of special arrangements, with colors indicated, for purses, bags, aprons and skirts, children's clothing, etc.

Huckaback Lace (Needham): Instructions; pattern analysis; diagrams and treadling; six-, eight-, and ten-harness; lace on tabby; lace on Huck; etc. With these instructions you can develop your own design. There are also three pages with specific designs.

Loom Lace (Needham): A number of the best and most attractive methods for producing a lace fabric without resort to finger manipulation. Bronson with variations; three-harness lace; Swedish lace; huck lace.

Rosepath Bouquet (Needham): Over 300 variations, including twills and overshots in color or texture effects; also complete instructions for working out original designs. Literally thousands of designs are possible using the methods outlined.

Silver Stars Sampler (Needham): An overshot study of an original miniature with instruction, including treadlings, for 24 techniques that can be used in overshot. Text describes change from basic treadling to rose fashion in three ways; honeycomb; shadow; bound weaving (several types); twills, pickup of design motif; linen and texture weaves; locked wefts. Swivel for overshot. (Added: "Some Ways with Overshot" and "Treadling Possibilities for Overshot.")

Introduction to Tarascan Lace (Newman): Instructions, explanation of peculiarities, diagrams for designs, alphabet, photo of samples, worksheet.

States of the Union (Newman): Direction for making drafts from name codes, and overshot drafts, with drawdowns, of names of all 50 states and the District of Columbia. Many of them were contributed by weavers for their favorite states.

Double-Width Weaving on the Eight-Harness Loom (Newman): Explanation of the making of the draft, the table of treadlings for four-harness weaves; six drafts with treadling; Bronson Runner; Border All Around; Mat in Bronson; also Turned Spot Bronson; Tray Cloth in M's and O's; Overshot (Honeysuckle); Huck Towel with checked border; Crackle, with directions for Circular Weaving; Rosepath Twill (no draft given).

Five-Block Diamond in Hand Weaving: Part I, Overshot (Margaret Newman): First of a series applying the diamond to all possible weaves. Under 22 headings, about 88 ways to weave Overshot; can be applied, with varying success, to any overshot draft. In addition there is an eight-harness Overshot Draft, with four ways to weave.

Two Harness Lace (Needham): Detailed instructions for the weaving of: Spanish Open Work, Bouquet, Leno Lace, Danish Medallion, and Two-Harness Bronson, with applications of each, directions for specific articles, and two pages of design motifs.

What Tabby Does to Overshot (Newman): Diagrams and explanations on the effect of opposite tabbies on Overshot weaving (or other weaves using tabby), with sample and several drafts with treadling illustrating the principle.

Music Drafts (Newman): Explicit instructions for making overshot drafts from music; ten such drafts, with drawdowns.

The Five-Block Diamond in Hand Weaving: Part II, Crackle (Newman):
Similar in form to *Part I, Overshot.*

Five-Block Diamond in Hand Weaving: Part III, Twills (Newman): Four-
harness and eight-harness Rosepath, treadling for Waffle for each. Six
drafts with twill directions, adapted to five-block diamond profile; and
12 tie-ups suitable for all drafts (except the four-harness Rosepath).

Five-Block Diamond in Hand Weaving: Part IV, Linen and Lace Weaves
(Newman): Barleycorn, Bronson, Finnish Lace, Huck, M's and O's,
Swedish Lace, Swedish Linen Weave (Step Twill).

Five-Block Diamond in Hand Weaving: Part V, Doubles (Newman):
Double Weave, Double Twill, Damask, Double Draft (Rosepath and
Overshot), Border All Around.

*Five-Block Diamond in Hand Weaving: Part VI, Summer and Winter and
Derivatives* (Newman): Summer and Winter and Ways to Weave; Double,
Bergman, Quigley, Bateman, Boulevard, Tag, Warp Stuffer.

Five-Block Diamond in Hand Weaving: Part VII, Warp Emphasis.
Comparison of four-harness and eight-harness; Shadow, Warp Face and
Log Cabin, Reserve Warp (Warp Pattern), and Pattern in Warp. Samples
extra. Announced for June 1975.

Five-Block Diamond in Hand Weaving: Part VIII, Miscellaneous.
Swivel Six-Harness, Honeycomb Four- and Eight-Harness; Saddle Blanket
Weave; Brocade; Ten-Harness (one from Henriksson, one from Syysale).

To quote from Ms. Newman, "The last four leaflets are tentative. I may find
a better subject than Summer and Winter—one on which there is less material
available."

51. Nye, Thelma M., ed. **Swedish Weaving.** New York, Van Nostrand Reinhold, 1972. 120p. illus. $8.95.

A perfectly marvelous book that even gives one a purchase source for the
yarns indicated. Clear directions are given for projects of all kinds—lamp
shades, tapestries, clothing, upholstery, and many more. Color plates, photographs, and black and white illustrations enhance the text, which is designed
to start the weaver thinking about original pieces. The experienced weaver
will be delighted with it, the beginner will have a high time browsing. There is
a chapter on looms, plus metric conversion tables for lengths and widths.
Another good book from Sweden, not yet translated but easily understood
with a Swedish dictionary, is *Handbok I Viving*, by Caroline Halvorsen
(J. W. Cappelens Forlag; distr. McMinnville, Ore., Robin and Russ Handweavers; $9.95). It gives about 200 patterns, plus information about equip-
ment and techniques. About one-half of the patterns are for four-harness looms
and the remainder are for from five to twelve harnesses.

52. Nyquist, Janet. **Speed Warping**. Storrs, Conn., Book Barn, 1972. 8p. illus. $2.95pa.

Most handloom weavers will get some tips here. Time-saving systems for warping are often discussed among weavers; it would be a shame to overlook new ideas just because one is wedded to a particular system. Ms. Nyquist says that one should aim at putting 471 warp ends through heddle eyes in one hour and ten minutes. Indeed a good time.

53. Oelsner, G. H. **Handbook of Weaves**. Rev. ed. by Samuel S. Dale. New York, Dover, 1951. 402p. illus. $7.50.

Originally published in 1915, this reprint has a lucid text supplemented by 1,875 working diagrams. It was written as a textbook for textile technicians, but it is of great use to the 8-, 12-, 16-, or 20-harness hand weaver. The serious, advanced weaver will want this book. If one thinks of a pattern, the chances are that Oelsner has it.

54. Overman, Ruth, and Lula Smith. **Contemporary Handweaving**. Ames, Iowa State University Press, 1955. 180p. illus. $7.50.

The basic book for four-harness weaving. Despite the fact that it unfortunately looks like a rather nondescript textbook, it is important. The beginning four-harness weaver could, by following the book carefully, warp and dress the loom without further instruction. There is a particularly good section on warping with a paddle. The illustrations follow the text well and, as the authors intended, the emphasis is on design and a creative approach to weaving. Regensteiner mentions this in her bibliography (entry 58), as does Znamierowski (entry 115).

55. Plath, Iona. **The Craft of Handweaving**. New York, Scribner's, 1972. 128p. illus. $3.95pa.

Please see the review below of *Handweaving*, published in 1964; this one is almost the same book. The illustrations, except the cover, are in black and white. The beginner as well as the experienced weaver will find it helpful and interesting. Ms. Plath explains that many four-harness weaves can be woven on a two-harness loom; although the book is designed mainly for four-harness looms, it also covers two, six, and eight harnesses. Ms. Plath has also published an excellent book, *The Decorative Arts of Sweden* (New York, Dover, 1965; 218p. illus. $3.50).

56. Plath, Iona. **Handweaving**. New York, Scribner's, 1964. 160p. illus. $8.95.

The 125 patterns are mainly for four-harness weavers, however, a few two-, six-, and eight-harness weaves are included. There are ideas for upholstery, decorative fabrics, curtains, draperies, place mats, fashion fabrics, rugs, and pillows, plus three pages of photographs showing the exact size of yarns. Ninety patterns are shown in full color in addition to the other illustrations and diagrams. This is a book for the serious student of weaving and it will be of particular interest to those interested in yardage. It is also useful for techniques and is altogether a beautiful work. Znamierowski (entry 115) and Justema (entry 339) find this a good source. There is a 1972 edition, only slightly different, called *The Craft of Handweaving* (see entry above).

57. Pyysalo, Helvi, and Vilvi Merisalo. **Handweaving Patterns from Finland.** Tr. by Bertha Needham and Aili Marsh. Newton Center, Mass., Branford, 1960. 56p. illus. $5.00.

Here is a wealth of information from Finland; the 122 complete projects include linens, draperies, upholstery, and wearing apparel. Full directions, a draft, and a photograph are included for each project. Regensteiner (entry 58) mentions this in her bibliography as do others.

58. Regensteiner, Else. **The Art of Weaving.** New York, Van Nostrand Reinhold, 1970. 184p. illus. $13.50.

Presenting a handsome survey for the beginner, Ms. Regensteiner touches on most aspects of loom weaving, looms, designing, and drafting. Although the presentation is rather haphazard—that is, the chapters do not seem to follow in logical order—the ideas and illustrations are exciting; this is one of the important new books in the field. Weavers and libraries will most certainly want this book in their collections. Four-harness weaving is given the most attention, but eight-harness is also discussed. The glossary is particularly good; the bibliography is rather out-of-date (that is, the editions given are often not the latest ones), and the book is indexed. An excellent and exciting browsing and reference tool for weavers.

59. Regensteiner, Else. **Weaving Course: Ideas and Techniques.** New York, Van Nostrand Reinhold (announced for spring 1975). 144p. illus. $14.95.

This book for the advanced weaver has projects for items such as home furnishings, clothing, wall hangings, sculptural weaving, and toys. The author hopes to stimulate ideas rather than to give precise recipes. If this book is as exciting as her last one, all weavers have a treat in store for them.

60. Selander, Malin. **Swedish Hand Weaving: Weaving Patterns.** Tr. by Alice Griswold and Karin Haskonsen. 2nd ed. Göteburg, Sweden, Wezäta Förlag, 1961. 120p. illus. $6.95.

Ms. Selander's guides to weaving patterns are exceedingly fine, as this one testifies. It describes 180 modern textiles; 133 of them are color grouped in 16 pages, while another 100 or so photos show patterns in detail. Tie-ups and treadling drafts, plus the most exact yarn and color descriptions, make this the perfect book for those who do not want to design a pattern themselves or for those who need inspiration. It is for the experienced weaver, but the beginner will want to browse. There are tablecloths, towels, pillow cases, curtains, draperies, upholstery, bedspreads, and rugs. Every textile shown is a delight to the eye. It is mostly for four-harness looms but there are a few patterns for multiharness looms.

61. Selander, Malin. **Swedish Swatches. Blue Series.** Göteborg, Sweden, Wezäta Förlag, 1969. 21p. illus. $12.95.

Detailed instructions (in English) and drafts accompany 20 actual swatches in this portfolio, which is intended to serve as a source of inspiration. These are mostly four-harness and eight-harness samples, but some six- and two-harness samples are also included. It would be hard to overstate the importance of Ms. Selander's contributions to weaving—and more particularly the importance of her "swatch books." The Yellow was published first, Blue followed, Red is just out (1974), and Green will be out in three years. If there is any way, see one of these books and buy it. Yellow is out of print, but it bears mentioning anyway. Dress, curtain, drape, coat, and upholstery fabrics are shown, but each swatch could be used for almost anything desired. The *Red Series* (1974; 21p.; $15.95) is magnificent.

62. Shillinglaw, Phyl. **Introducing Weaving.** New York, Watson-Guptill, 1972. 80p. illus. $7.95.

This really is an introduction to weaving. Not actually a how-to-do-it book, it will be useful as a source of ideas or stimulation. The novice and experienced weaver will find it exciting to experiment with raw and dyed fleece and other fibers, and the author presents her ideas on working with fleece. The many photographs of work by children are delightful. In the main, the book is designed for teachers.

63. **Shuttlecraft Guild Monographs.** Pacific Grove, Calif., Craft and Hobby, 1957– ; repr. Santa Ana, Calif., HTH Publishers, 1974.

These were put out by Harriet Tidball, who wrote many of them and edited the rest. The individual monographs are all found here. The *Shuttlecraft Guild Monographs* are as important today as they were when they were published. Weavers of every level will be interested in them; most of the writing, however, assumes that the user can read a draft. The beginning weaver can use them for an understanding of weaving. These monographs were originally published in two editions, one with swatches and the other not. (The reprint edition does not have swatches.) Every weaver must be aware of these monographs as a unique and valuable contribution to the art. Each monograph has a discussion, instructions, diagrams and drafts, plus, of course, much more. Many of the titles were out of print. However, the publishers, of Santa Ana, California, recently published a reprint edition of the whole series (entries 64-90). HTH is also reprinting many of the *Shuttlecraft Guild Bulletins*, excellent publications that every weaver should see.

64. Tidball, Harriet. **The Double Weave**. Pacific Grove, Calif., Craft and Hobby, 1960; repr. Santa Ana, Calif., HTH Publishers, 1974. 34p. illus. $4.50pa.

Shuttlecraft Guild Monograph No. 1 *Double Weave* is known as one of Ms. Tidball's best monographs. It is an excellent study of the many structures of double weave, including double-width cloth, shaping on the loom, and pick up techniques such as Finn weave. Although the book deals mainly with four-harness drafts and tie-ups, the weaver with more harnesses should study this monograph for information on double weave. Novices will want to browse, but experience is needed before one can use the book.

65. Tidball, Harriet. **Surface Interest: Textiles of Today**. Pacific Grove, Calif., Craft and Hobby, 1961; repr. Santa Ana, Calif., HTH Publishers, 1974. 22p. illus. $3.50pa.

Shuttlecraft Guild Monograph No. 2. This monograph is for experienced four-harness (or more) handweavers, but everyone will find it interesting. The monograph deals with making fabrics with specialty yarns on the surface and other yarns as a firm base below. Forty-four designs are given for attractive fabrics. The complete instructions for each design include yarns, warp setts, sleys, warping, and finishing. This is an imaginative way to stretch those expensive yarns for yardage.

66. Atwater, Mary Meigs. **Design and Handweaver**. Pacific Grove, Calif., Craft and Hobby, 1961; repr. Santa Ana, Calif., HTH Publishers, 1974. 26p. illus. $3.50pa.

Shuttlecraft Monograph No. 3. Elements of design, proportion, texture, color, and pattern are given in a well-done monograph by the "dean of American handweavers."

67. Tidball, Harriet. **Woolens and Tweeds**. Pacific Grove, Calif., Craft and Hobby, 1961; repr. Santa Ana, Calif., HTH Publishers, 1974. 46p. illus. $4.50pa.

Shuttlecraft Guild Monograph No. 4. Ms. Tidball covers the history, the wool fiber (from fleece to woolen yarn), weaving woolens and finishing, and designing for woolens and tweeds. A necessary book for anyone working in this area.

68. Tidball, Harriet. **The Weaver's Book of Scottish Tartans.** Pacific Grove, Calif., Craft and Hobby, 1962; repr. Santa Ana, Calif., HTH Publishers, 1974. 46p. illus. $4.50pa.

Shuttlecraft Guild Monograph No. 5. As a preface to the directions for weaving a tartan, the pamphlet begins with a brief but nicely done history of the Scottish tartan, colors, and patterns. The how-to section is clearly illustrated and has a well-written text. Forty-six tartan terms, 260 setts, and the profiles of numerous clan tartans with their specific colors are combined to make a fascinating book for the experienced weaver who would like to weave a tartan. References and bibliography of sources are given.

69. Tidball, Harriet. **Mexican Motifs.** Pacific Grove, Calif., Craft and Hobby, 1962; repr. Santa Ana, Calif., HTH Publishers, 1974. 22p. illus. $3.50pa.

Shuttlecraft Guild Monograph No. 6. Covers Mexican Quesquimitl, 3-shaft warp face weave, leno or gauze weave, cotton warp-pattern fabric, vaxaca belts, and Mexican commercial handweaving. Combine the patterns, drafts and illustrations, a little bit of travelog, and you have an exciting monograph. Also included is a rather fine discussion of the backstrap loom, its possibilities for the modern weaver, and how it functions. This book is for all weavers interested in Mexico, in backstrap weaving, or in using these techniques on any loom.

70. Tidball, Harriet. **Contemporary Satins.** Pacific Grove, Calif., Craft and Hobby, 1962; repr. Santa Ana, Calif., HTH Publishers, 1974. 33p. illus. $4.50pa.

Shuttlecraft Guild Monograph No. 7. Imagine place mats or upholstery or luncheon cloths in an attractive, contemporary design and texture and also in satin weave. Ms. Tidball again presents a standard weave in a new setting. She treats the history, the satin interval, drafting, threading, treadling, compound and irregular satins, damask, three-block patterns, designing, and technical problems clearly and carefully. The fabrics were done by various weavers. An experienced weaver would probably have better luck using this as a text, but the beginner will enjoy browsing.

71. Collingwood, Peter. **Peter Collingwood: His Weaves and Weaving.** Pacific Grove, Calif., Craft and Hobby, 1963; repr. Santa Ana, Calif., HTH Publishers, 1974. 46p. illus. $4.50pa.

Shuttlecraft Guild Monograph No. 8. An expert presents practical hints plus information on rug designing, finishing, knotting, and ikat dyeing used in handweaving rugs. Some of Mr. Collingwood's original techniques are described here—for instance, the double woven corduroy, a flat weave without tabby, and, as a surprise, directions for tying up a double counter-march loom. He does not stop at rugs, however. There are instructions for a jacket with sleeves woven in only two pieces, as well as other patterns.

72. Tidball, Harriet. **Undulating Weft Effects**. Pacific Grove, Calif., Craft and Hobby, 1963; repr. Santa Ana, Calif., HTH Publishers, 1974. 27p. illus. $4.50pa.

Shuttlecraft Guild Monograph No. 9. Another weaver's delight. Ms. Tidball's work on Honeycomb is beautifully detailed and pays great attention to actual needs. These monographs are meant for the experienced weaver, but this is not to say that the beginner cannot gain knowledge to be used later. It is mostly geared to the four harness hand weaver, but weavers with larger looms will also benefit. Covered in this monograph are the history, characteristics, functional uses, colors, warp and weft controls, and drafts of Honeycomb, plus curly weave, spider weave, borders, and much more. An important work.

73. Tidball, Harriet. **Merry Christmas, Handweavers**. Pacific Grove, Calif., Craft and Hobby, 1963; repr. Santa Ana, Calif., HTH Publishers, 1974. 38p. illus. $3.50pa.

Shuttlecraft Guild Monograph No. 10. A particularly merry monograph showing delightful ideas for creating Christmas cards and decorations using handwoven fabrics.

74. Tidball, Harriet. **Handwoven Specialties**. Pacific Grove, Calif., Craft and Hobby, 1964; repr. Santa Ana, Calif., HTH Publishers, 1974. 38p. illus. $4.50pa.

Shuttlecraft Guild Monograph No. 11. Here are 62 articles for the handweaver to make, including pillow covers, purses, book jackets, covered boxes, closet accessories, sofa throws, and others, each with clear, careful directions and photographs. Having this many nice ideas in one pamphlet makes it a good buy for the weaver with some experience. One can use already woven fabrics for some of the items or weave new ones.

75. Tidball, Harriet. **Contemporary Tapestry**. Pacific Grove, Calif., Craft and Hobby, 1964; repr. Santa Ana, Calif., HTH Publishers, 1974. 81p. illus. $6.00pa.

Shuttlecraft Guild Monograph No. 12. This is one of the best texts available on tapestry. Modern woven tapestry is covered rather completely, and the good illustrations include photographs of types of looms and tools. The narrative is easy to follow, with sections on tapestry composition, tapestry techniques, and cartoon drawing. Many of the tapestries are modern indeed, with open warps and textured effects. Finishing is also discussed. A novice can use this easily, but the more experienced weaver will also enjoy it. The text was taken from a workshop by Eva Antilla.

76. Tidball, Harriet. **Thomas Jackson, Weaver.** Pacific Grove, Calif., Craft and Hobby, 1964; repr. Santa Ana, Calif., HTH Publishers, 1974. 37p. illus. $4.50pa.

Shuttlecraft Guild Monograph No. 13. Records from the seventeenth and eighteenth century are reproduced here. The Jackson family of Yorkshire, England, were weavers and kept notebooks of their work. These record books, now at Cooper Union Museum in New York City, were the basis for this monograph.

77. Rhodes, Tonya. **Color Related Decorating Textiles: Rugs, Upholstery, Drapery.** Pacific Grove, Calif., Craft and Hobby, 1965; repr. Santa Ana, Calif., HTH Publishers, 1974. $4.50pa.

Shuttlecraft Guild Monograph No. 14. Presents 72 window and upholstery fabrics in four coordinated color groups for the weaver. Useful and interesting.

78. Atwater, Mary Meigs. **Guatemala Visited.** Pacific Grove, Calif., Craft and Hobby, 1965; repr. Santa Ana, Calif., HTH Publishers, 1974. 46p. illus. $4.50pa.

Shuttlecraft Guild Monograph No. 15. A personal view of a trip to Guatemala; includes the kind of description of design and color, with detailed diagrams and instructions, that one would expect from Ms. Atwater.

79. Tidball, Harriet. **Color and Dyeing.** Pacific Grove, Calif., Craft and Hobby, 1965; repr. Santa Ana, Calif., HTH Publishers, 1974. 53p. illus. $6.00pa.

Shuttlecraft Guild Monograph No. 16. A detailed treatment of color and dyeing for the handweaver. All the instructions are here for the beginner.

80. Tidball, Harriet. **Supplemental Warp Patterning.** Pacific Grove, Calif., Craft and Hobby, 1966; repr. Santa Ana, Calif., HTH Publishers, 1974. 46p. illus. $4.50pa.

Shuttlecraft Guild Monograph No. 17. Using a supplementary warp gives many possible pattern elements; this monograph explores the possibilities in depth. It gives instructions for looms of two to sixteen harnesses.

81. Tidball, Harriet. **Textile Structure and Analysis.** Pacific Grove, Calif., Craft and Hobby, 1966; repr. Santa Ana, Calif., HTH Publishers, 1974. 30p. illus. $4.50pa.

Shuttlecraft Guild Monograph No. 18. A home study course for four-harness, or multiharness weavers who want to know more about textile structure and analysis. The 30 pages of detailed instructions, with many photographs, form the substance for 12 separate lessons. A new way to study textile structure—weaving diagrams on cards rather than drawing them—is described and analyzed. The course plan assumes experience on the weaver's part. This would make a nice guild study group course. It is the quality one associates with Shuttlecraft Guild Monographs. The Draft Form pads are now available as a separate publication for $3.50 (3 pads for $15.00) from HTH.

82. Tidball, Harriet. **Summer and Winter: And Other Two-Tie Unit Weaves.** Pacific Grove, Calif., Craft and Hobby, 1966; repr. Santa Ana, Calif., HTH Publishers, 1974. 58p. illus. $6.00pa.

Shuttlecraft Guild Monograph No. 19. Summer and Winter, historically and in the present, is one of the most important weaves for the four- (and more) harness weaver. It is presented here, not only with complete, comprehensive directions for the basic weave, but with the infinite variations possible. The numerous clear illustrations include both diagrams and photographs. The endless possibilities and the enduring beauty of Summer and Winter explain its continued popularity. Ms. Tidball has done full justice to it. The weaver will have to have experience reading drafts to use this book, but it is basic to any weaving library.

83. Tidball, Harriet. **Two-Harness Textiles: The Loom Controlled Weaves.** Pacific Grove, Calif., Craft and Hobby, 1967; repr. Santa Ana, Calif., HTH Publishers, 1974. 30p. illus. $4.50pa.

Shuttlecraft Guild Monograph No. 20. This monograph discusses loom-controlled weaves for decorative effects covered in later monographs. An excellent reference tool.

84. Tidball, Harriet. **Two-Harness Textiles: The Open-Work Weaves.** Pacific Grove, Calif., Craft and Hobby, 1967; repr. Santa Ana, Calif., HTH Publishers, 1974. 34p. illus. $4.50pa.

Shuttlecraft Guild Monograph No. 21. A discussion of the open-work, hand-manipulated weaves for patterns. Another excellent reference tool.

85. Tidball, Harriet. **Brocade.** Pacific Grove, Calif., Craft and Hobby, 1967; repr. Santa Ana, Calif., HTH Publishers, 1974. 50p. illus. $6.00pa.

Shuttlecraft Guild Monograph No. 22. Develops brocade patterns, both traditional and modern, for the experienced weaver. One of the numerous Tidball monographs, this one is well done from every point of view, as might be expected. The weaver is encouraged to use imagination and create his own design in brocade. Regensteiner, among others, lists it in her bibliography (entry 58).

86. Tidball, Harriet. **Build or Buy a Loom: Patterns for Pickups.** Pacific Grove, Calif., Craft and Hobby, 1968; repr. Santa Ana, Calif., HTH Publishers, 1974. 25p. illus. $4.50pa.

Shuttlecraft Guild Monograph No. 23. Two short publications have been combined here to make a publication large enough to be called a monograph. The first is a fine discussion of a number of looms, covering the many points that the reader should consider before investing in a loom (e.g., the uses the loom will be put to, and which loom is the most practical for a given use). Specific plans are included for building a two-harness loom. The second section, on pick-up patterns or brocade, will be very interesting to the weaver with some experience. Many good practice patterns are given for looms with two to eight harnesses. Ms. Tidball does not recommend free designing at the loom while a weave is being mastered.

87. Tidball, Harriet. **Contemporary Costume: Strictly Handwoven to Wear.** Pacific Grove, Calif., Craft and Hobby, 1968; repr. Santa Ana, Calif., HTH Publishers, 1974. 44p. illus. $6.00pa.

Shuttlecraft Guild Monograph No. 24. Few texts are devoted to weaving and shaping articles of clothing on the loom. Ms. Tidball shows an evening skirt, hostess pajamas, a fringed coat, a double weave coat, a round cape and others. There are patterns, directions, diagrams, and photographs, plus suggestions for the finishing touches. The work, which represents the combined efforts of three weavers, was edited by Ms. Tidball. Most of the fashions are timeless in design. One should also see Wilson's *Weaving You Can Wear* (entry 113).

88. Tidball, Harriet. **Peru: Textiles Unlimited, Part I and Part II.** Pacific Grove, Calif., Craft and Hobby, 1969; repr. Santa Ana, Calif., HTH Publishers, 1974. 2 pts. illus. $4.50pa. ea.

Shuttlecraft Guild Monographs No. 25 and 26. Part I deals with history and general information, while Part II is mostly technical information for the experienced weaver. Drafts and weaving methods of ancient Peru are discussed in detail, including weft face plain weave, structural weft, three-color warp pattern pick-up, fringes and tabs, gauze and filet, and much more. Photographs supplement the how-to-do-it text. Specific recommendations for yarn and warp setts are avoided, so that the weaver can have freedom of expression. More information on these techniques is in *The Weaver's Book* by Tidball (entry 100).

89. Tidball, Harriet. **Weaving Inkle Bands.** Pacific Grove, Calif., Craft and Hobby, 1969; repr. Santa Ana, Calif., HTH Publishers, 1974. 24p. illus. $4.50pa.

Shuttlecraft Guild Monograph No. 27. This completely rewritten edition of an earlier book by Ms. Tidball shows her usual attention to detail. There are directions for constructing (in a home workshop) several types of inkle looms. Patterns and drafts are given for belts, bags, handles, tubes, guitar straps, and many more items that can be woven on this sort of narrow loom.

90. Harvey, Virginia, and Harriet Tidball. **Weft Twining.** Pacific Grove, Calif., Craft and Hobby, 1969; repr. Santa Ana, Calif., HTH Publishers, 1974. 39p. illus. $4.50pa.

Shuttlecraft Guild Monograph No. 28. This monograph, the last, was finished by Virginia Harvey after Ms. Tidball's death. There is a history of weft twining, a discussion of where it has been used, definitions, and projects. A valuable work by two authorities.

91. Simpson, L. E., and N. Weir. **The Weaver's Craft.** 9th rev. ed. Leicester, England, Dryad Press; Peoria, Ill., Manual Arts Press, 1965. 198p. illus. $5.95pa.

This comprehensive account of weaving in various forms and materials has passed through many editions. From the simplest felt and raffia weaving for small children to complex floor looms, this book covers all aspects in detail. There are sections on spinning and dyeing the wool, color, pattern drafting, analysis of fabrics, specific patterns for weaving, and finishing of tweeds. The history of weaving is presented throughout the book.

92. Snow, Edith Huntington, and Laura L. Peasley. **Weaving Lessons for Handlooms.** Swarthmore, Pa., Marguerite P. Davison, n.d. illus. $2.50 pa.

Primarily a book for beginners. The authors wrote it as a text for their students when they were leaving them for a period of study abroad. It would be quite suitable for guild use. Basic information on looms, equipment, warping, dressing the loom, selecting the thread and pattern, and weaving. The directions and accompanying illustrations are clear.

93. Snyder, Mary E. **The Crackle Weave**. Repr. Avon, Conn., Book Barn, 1973. 56p. illus. $3.50pa.

This excellent, carefully detailed, how-to-do-it book is ideal for the experienced weaver. It would make a perfect lesson plan for a guild study program. The 42 projects are arranged to introduce and instruct the weaver in the design possibilities of crackle weave. Traditional, contemporary, multi-harness, ecclesiastical—all are included. Crackle weave is not very well known, which makes the idea of this book even more interesting.

94. Snyder, Mary E. **Lace and Lacey Weaves**. Repr. Avon, Conn., Book Barn, 1973. 64p. illus. $3.50pa.

Lace and Lacey Weaves covers Bronson lace on 4, 6, 8, and 11 harnesses, Swedish lace, barley corn, diaper, canvas weaves, 27 samples of pick-up lace, and others too numerous to mention. Ms. Snyder has divided the book into five lesson plans that cover 47 lace and lacey projects. Like her other book, this one is a source for all weavers, including novices with some experience. It would also be a good home or guild study course. Ms. Snyder is well-known for her workshops; she speaks from experience.

95. Snyder, Mary. **Scottish District Checks**. Pasadena, Calif., Snyder, 1965; distr. McMinnville, Ore., Robin and Russ Handweavers, 1965. 26p. $2.00pa.

These district checks were collected and compiled from a study group working under Ms. Snyder's tutelage in 1965. It is unique simply because these are quite difficult to locate elsewhere. There are complete directions for setts and yarns for 91 different checks for four-harness looms. No photographs are included, but the working directions are sufficient. For experienced floor loom weavers.

96. Thorpe, Azalea, and Jack L. Larsen. **Elements of Weaving**. Ed. by Mary Lyon. Garden City, N.Y., Doubleday, 1967. 257p. illus. $9.95.

A complete introduction to the craft of handweaving from the most fundamental principles of simple looms and elementary weaves to more advanced textile designs. Black and white plates. Written by two outstanding authorities, this is a basic book for handweavers. Regensteiner, among others, lists it in her bibliography (entry 58).

97. Thorpe, Heather G. **A Handweaver's Workbook**. 2nd ed. New York, Macmillan, 1966. 228p. illus. $4.95.

Easily followed step-by-step directions for weaving on the four-harness foot-treadle or hand operated loom. Good illustrations and many diagrams supplement the text. The author has included a section on types of looms to buy as well as a description of the parts of the loom and directions for weaving. The book is designed for interested beginners as well as for more experienced weavers who need a refresher.

98. Tidball, Harriet. **Handloom Weaves.** Pacific Grove, Calif., Craft and Hobby, 1957; repr. Santa Ana, Calif., HTH Publishers, 1974. 38p. illus. $4.50pa.

This is an analysis (in draft and photograph) and classification of the 52 most important harness controlled weaves. Ms. Tidball tries in this book to establish a common terminology that would be acceptable to all handweavers. Weavers who need to read drafts from many places have long been plagued by the problem of terminologies and symbols that are entirely different. All experienced weavers who need to know more about the technical aspects of weaving will need this basic text.

99. Tidball, Harriet, and Harriet C. Douglas. **Handweaver's Instruction Manual.** Pacific Grove, Calif., Craft and Hobby, 1967. 42p. illus. $3.00pa.

This standard text for handweavers contains good, basic information on equipment, warping, weaving techniques, and reading and developing drafts. Fifty-six drafts are shown. The authors' purpose was to give enough basic information to enable the weaver to become independent and more creative. The book would be suitable not only for novices but also for the more experienced who lack some of the basic techniques.

100. Tidball, Harriet. **The Weaver's Book: Fundamentals of Handweaving.** New York, Macmillan, 1961. 173p. illus. $5.95.

A necessary book for the beginner and all other weavers, by one of the best and most prolific writers of books on handweaving and allied crafts. The text presents basic information that every weaver could use from time to time such as yardage needed for fabrics (for clothing and household), the size of household articles, and warp setts for cotton, linen, and wool. In addition, it deals with preparation of the loom and all weave classes. This is an excellent reference tool for all floor loom weavers. And it is a basic text for the Tidball Shuttlecraft Guild Monograph No. 18, *Textile Structure and Analysis.* It is for four-harness looms only, but the information is basic and can be extended. By all means, buy it. Indexed.

101. Tod, Osma Gallinger. **Booklet of Belt Weaves.** Coral Gables, Fla., the author, n.d. $2.00pa.

Like Ms. Tod's other books and pamphlets, this one is well done. They are available through her studio as well as through other outlets. Some of her other titles are *Hints for the Handweaver* ($2.50); *75 Original Bertha Hayes*

Drafts ($4.00); and *Complete Book of Bertha Hayes Patterns* (57p., illus., $4.25pa.). Ms. Tod performed a real service for weavers by publishing the 75 drafts and designs created by Bertha Hayes and the complete patterns of Bertha Hayes.

102. Tod, Osma Gallinger. **The Joy of Handweaving**. 2nd ed. New York, Bonanza, 1964. 326p. illus. $7.95.

A book for beginners that will also serve the more experienced. Here is a history of handweaving, an explanation of the fundamentals of weaving and all basic weaves, an extensive thread chart, and a group of projects that will interest weavers at all levels. Znamierowski and Regensteiner (entries 115 and 58), among others, mention this book in their bibliographies. It could easily be one of the first purchased by a weaver. Although the author deals mainly with four-harness, she also discusses two-harness and even touches on eight. It has a glossary, a bibliography, and an index.

103. Tod, Osma Gallinger, and Josephine del Deo. **Rug Weaving for Everyone**. New York, Bramhall House, 1957. 294p. illus. $3.95.

Traditional and contemporary rugs are discussed here, with clear, well-illustrated directions for almost every kind of rug weaving. The 138 illustrations (black and white and in color) aid the user. Both the novice and the experienced weaver will find projects of interest. Ms. Tod is a well-known weaver and writer on weaving. For a Navajo rug one would want to consult Noël Bennett's work (entry 119) or Mary Pendleton's (entry 126).

104. Tovey, John. **The Technique of Weaving**. New York, Reinhold, 1965. 128p. illus. $7.95.

A thorough treatment for those interested enough in weaving to want to read and understand more. Beginners and intermediates could benefit. Subjects covered within this book are looms, loom preparation, weaving, and specialized techniques. There are 225 illustrations supplementing the text. Ms. Regensteiner, as well as others, lists this in her bibliography (entry 58).

105. Tovey, John. **Weaves and Pattern Drafting**. New York, Reinhold, 1969. 96p. illus. $7.95.

Numerous line drawings and photographs accompany the concise text in this discussion of creative possibilities for the intermediate or advanced weaver. Also included are loom modifications for extra warp or gauze. Mr. Tovey is a lecturer at the Regional College of Art, Kingston-Upon-Hill, England. This book is a basic text for all loom weavers. Bibliography and index.

106. Waller, Irene. **Designing with Thread: From Fiber to Fabric**. New York, Viking, 1973. 183p. illus. $14.95.

Another unique book that takes the student beyond how-to-do-it to what to do and why. It explores the relationship between the artist and industry, and also discusses design; hand spinning and machine spinning; how, when, and with what to dye; how to finish and present works; machine knitting; and more. The author, a British production designer and an exhibiting artist, has produced an exceptional work for the serious student—a book, in fact, that has long been needed. It is an exciting work that should find its way into all libraries.

107. Watson, William. **Advanced Textile Design**. London, Longman, 1955. 519p. illus. $16.50.

Another title (his first was *Textile Design and Color*) by a major writer on textile design. Mr. Watson's books are mentioned by both Ms. Znamierowski (entry 115) and Ms. Regensteiner (entry 58) in their bibliographies on design in weaving. This book deals in particular with the systems of designing, plus a description of the special jacquard and loom mountings used in producing the fabrics. Chapters include backed cloths, double cloths, treble cloths, extra weft and warp figuring, figured muslin and damask, tapestry and upholstery, quilts, gauze and leno, lappet weaving and designing, swivel weaving, Turkish toweling and more. More than 500 illustrations aid the user. Both of Watson's books continue to be of the greatest importance in the field of textile design. They fall into the category of must items for anyone interested in designing and weaving textiles.

108. West, Virginia M. **Finishing Touches for the Handweaver**. Newton Centre, Mass., Branford, 1967. 102p. illus. $5.75.

The author gives instructions for various methods of finishing articles, covering such techniques as fringes, hemstitching, fagoting, embroidery, and how to secure corners. Regensteiner mentions this rather unique and very useful book in her bibliography (entry 58). Diagrams and photographs illustrate the instructions well. The entire book is clear and helpful; it will probably serve as a basic tool. Even if it is not needed for that purpose, it will furnish ideas. *Finishing Touches* will be useful to everyone.

109. Willcox, Donald J. **Techniques of Rya Knotting**. New York, Van Nostrand Reinhold, 1971. 136p. illus. $8.95.

A picture book with instructions for weavers who intend to pursue the rya technique and also for those only interested in reading about it. The history of rya is illustrated with over 100 photographs taken in Scandinavia. The section on hand knotting pile onto a fabric background presents a technique that beginners can easily do. In the discussion of knotting on the loom (true rya), however, the author assumes that the reader is already familiar with basic weaving techniques. The book successfully extends the weaver's thinking about rya and opens new horizons for rya creations. A Finnish book, *Ryyy*, by Annikki Toikka-Karvonen (Helsinki, Kustannusosakeyhtio Otava, 1971; 522p., illus.; $64.00) is a handsome and comprehensive treatment of the history of rya. Any weaver interested in rya would do well to see a copy. It is in Finnish but an English summary is available.

110. Wilson, Jean. **The Pile Weaves: Twenty-Six Techniques and How to Do Them.** New York, Van Nostrand Reinhold, 1974. 96p. illus. $5.95; $2.95pa.

Pile weaves for added warmth, color, texture, and dimension for rugs, carpets, cushions, and wall hangings are described here by a major writer, weaver, and teacher. It is well written and illustrated and nicely planned, as are the rest of Ms. Wilson's books on handweaving.

111. Wilson, Jean. **Weaving Is Creative: The Weaver-Controlled Weaves.** New York, Van Nostrand Reinhold, 1973. 268p. illus. $14.95.

Another excellent book in the "Weaving Is" series that will interest all weavers. This particular work was the outgrowth of a year's study by the Seattle Weaver's Guild. The beginning tapestry weaver will be helped by the photographs and diagrams of the weaves. Everyone will benefit from the discussions of joinings, fringes, twining and chaining, brocade and pick-up weaves. An unusual and valuable aid is the notebook at the end of each section, diagramming the technique and telling more about it. Although Ms. Wilson designed this third book to help experienced weavers develop creativity, it will be equally useful and necessary to novices. Glossary, index, and bibliography are included.

112. Wilson, Jean. **Weaving You Can Use.** New York, Van Nostrand Reinhold (announced for Spring 1975). 104p. illus. $14.95.

Another useful Jean Wilson book for handweavers. The projects include items for the home such as rugs, table settings, baby carriers, upholstery, pillows, and much more. Basic loom-shaped forms, the rectangle and the circle, are employed in a majority of the projects. It is intended as a sequel to *Weaving You Can Wear* (entry 113).

113. Wilson, Jean, with Jan Burhen. **Weaving You Can Wear.** New York, Van Nostrand Reinhold, 1973. 128p. illus. $8.95; $4.95pa.

Men, women, and children can use these exciting ethnic garments and interesting belts, pockets, bags, umbrellas, and collars. The shaping of the items is simple, based usually on the square or rectangle. The item comes off the loom almost ready to be used. The authors assume that the reader can already weave, and many decisions (weight, type of thread, color, etc.) are left to the weaver. But patterns, finishing stitches, and a multitude of ideas are here to provide inspiration. Weavers and anyone interested in learning to weave should invest in this excellent book, and libraries should also have this book in their collections. *Creating Body Covering*, by Jean Ray Laury and Joyce Aiken (New York, Van Nostrand Reinhold, 1973; 152p., illus.; $4.95pa.), is a fascinating new book with good pictures. It covers embroidery, printed and painted fabrics, fibers, applique, tie-dye and batik, leather, weaving, non-clothing, patchwork, and accessories.

114. Zielinski, S. **Encyclopedia of Handweaving.** New York, Funk and Wagnalls, 1959. 190p. illus. $8.50.

A basic work for any library whose patrons are interested in weaving. All terms are explained from a weaver's point of view. Topics are arranged first in broad categories (tools, theory, operation, raw materials, patterns, fabrics), then subdivided. Consequently, the user can search for a word or process through more than one avenue. Regensteiner (entry 58) lists this work in her bibliography, as do Justema (entry 339) and others. Don't overlook the browsing aspect of this superior reference tool. All in all, it is a stimulating book.

115. Znamierowski, Nell. **Step-by-Step Weaving: A Complete Introduction to the Craft of Weaving.** New York, Golden Press, 1967. 96p. illus. $2.50pa.

Here in an inexpensive but very good introduction to looms, weaving, and finishing. The marvelous illustrations lead the reader through the projects chosen by the author, but there is also guidance for those who want to create their own projects. It is difficult to praise this book enough as an aid for the beginner and also to help the teacher answer frequently raised questions. Coverage ranges from simple through four-harness looms, and there is even a section on dyeing. The author has included a bibliography and lists of suppliers of yarns, looms, equipment, and dyes. Also of interest is a directory of schools.

NORTH AMERICAN INDIAN WEAVING

116. Amsden, Charles A. **Navajo Weaving: Its Technique and History.** Santa Ana, Calif., The Fine Arts Press, 1934. Repr. in cooperation with the Southwest Museum of Fine Arts, Los Angeles. Original color plate linoleum blocks supplied by the University of New Mexico Press, 1964, and published by Rio Grande Press, Glorieta, New Mexico, 1972. 262p. illus. $12.00.

The reprinting of this excellent anthropological study of Navajo weaving was a significant event for anyone interested in the art of the Indians in the Southwest. In this classic volume, Amsden provides a detailed study of the design, materials, and weaving techniques of the Navajo Indians, relating this art form to their religious and cultural history. For a fuller picture, the person seriously interested in the Navajo ought to also read both of Gladys Reichard's books (see entries 127, 128) one of which was published the same year as Amsden's. Both have also been reprinted. The illustrations provided by Amsden are of great value to both the weaver and the student of Navajo culture. This basic work is listed in every bibliography that touches on the history and culture of the Navajo Indians.

117. Bennett, Noël. **Are You Sure?** Santa Fe, N.M., Museum of Ceremonial Art, 1973. 21p. illus. $1.15pa.

Buying a Navajo rug? Reading this pamphlet will help you buy a true Navajo and not a copy. The differences are described, and seven black and white photographs accompany the narrative. Ms. Bennett is exceptionally well qualified to write this pamphlet; she has spent years studying and weaving Navajo rugs, writing about them, and teaching others about them.

118. Bennett, Noël. **The Weavers Pathway: A Clarification of the Spirit-Trail in Navajo Weaving.** Flagstaff, Ariz., Northland Press, 1973. 104p. illus. $8.95.

Noël Bennett's newest book on Navajo weaving is beautifully done, as befits the subject, and is sensitively written, as one would expect from the author. This is not a how-to-do-it (as was her *Working with the Wool*, entry 119), but an explanation of the "Spirit Trail" (the thread path) used in Navajo weaving. This book is a service to those interested in Navajo rugs because a great deal of misinformation on this subject has been circulated in the past. Illustrations abound, as do quotes from authorities on and off the reservation. The bibliography is excellent.

119. Bennett, Noël, and Tiana Bighorse. **Working with the Wool: How to Weave a Navajo Rug.** Flagstaff, Ariz., Northland Press, 1971. 105p. illus. $8.00; $4.95pa.

The fine drawings by Robert Jacobson illustrate a thoughtfully prepared text by two unusually well-qualified authors. The step-by-step instructions tell one how to build a loom, how to warp it, and how to weave on it. In each section there is an exact list of supplies needed. Every technique is fully explored, as are problems that could arise. There is a good list of supply sources, a glossary of terms, and a list of suggested readings. All in all, an excellent book for someone who wishes to weave using Navajo techniques.

120. Dutton, Bertha P. **Navajo Weaving Today**. Santa Fe, N.M., Museum of New Mexico Press, 1961. 37p. illus. $1.45pa.

A factual presentation by a reputable writer. The pamphlet is entirely in black and white, however, which detracts from its usefulness. G. Maxwell (entry 125) or K. Kent (entry 124) would be more suitable for most book collections and certainly for libraries.

121. Hunt, W. Ben. **Complete How-To Book of Indiancraft**. New York, Collier Books, Macmillan, 1973. 187p. illus. $2.95.

Although it is not mainly on weaving, this book does contain some material on the subject that will be interesting to craft teachers, group leaders, and others. The author, now in his nineties, has written a number of books over the past decades; this one is a refining and combining of those texts.

122. **Indian Leaflet Series**. Denver, Colo., Denver Art Museum, 1930 , reprints from 1967). $0.15ea.

Each of these authoritative, four-page leaflets has an excellent bibliography. Frederic Douglas was the Curator of Indian Art at the Museum for many years, and his publications in the field are widely recognized for their accuracy. The following issues of the series are applicable to this bibliography:

No. 1, *Northwest Coast Indians*. By F. H. Douglas. 1930; 2nd ed. 1937; repr. 1967. Contains paragraphs on weaving and dyeing.

No. 3, *Navajo Spinning, Dyeing, and Weaving*. By Jean Allard Jeançon and F. H. Douglas. 1930; repr. 1971.

No. 18, *Hopi Indian Weaving*. By Jean Allard Jeançcon and F. H. Douglas. 1931; repr. 1971.

Nos. 59 and 60, *Indian Cloth-Making: Looms, Techniques and Kinds of Fabrics*. By F. H. Douglas. 1933; repr. 1968.

No. 63, *Indian Vegetable Dyes: Part 1*. By Jessie Matson and F. H. Douglas. 1934; repr. 1969.

No. 71, *Indian Vegetable Dyes: Part 2*. By Mona Hanks and F. H. Douglas. 1936; repr. 1968.

No. 89, *Acoma Pueblo Weaving and Embroidery*. By F. H. Douglas. 1939; repr. 1967.

No. 90, *Weaving in the Tewa Puebloes*. By F. H. Douglas. 1939; repr. 1967.

No. 91, *Weaving of the Keres Pueblos and Weaving of the Tiwa Pueblos and Jemez*. By F. H. Douglas. 1939; repr. 1967.

Nos. 92 and 93, *Main Types of Pueblo Cotton Textiles.* By F. H. Douglas. 1940; repr. 1957.

Nos. 94 and 95, *Main Types of Pueblo Woolen Textiles.* By F. H. Douglas. 1940; repr. 1955.

Nos. 96 and 97, *Weaving at Zuni Pueblo.* By F. H. Douglas. 1940; repr. 1968.

No. 116, *Southwestern Weaving Materials.* By F. H. Douglas. 1953; repr. 1957.

123. James, George Wharton. **Indian Blankets and Their Makers.** Glorieta, N.M., Rio Grande Press, 1973; repr. of 1927 edition. 213p. illus. $20.00. Also reprinted New York, Dover, 1974. $5.00.

Mr. James considered his books to be works of love; the Rio Grande Press is doing a service by reprinting many of these good older titles—including Reichard (entries 127-28) and Amsden (entry 116). Pueblo and Navajo blankets are discussed in detail, and many are shown in color. There is also an excellent map of the areas of production. Mr. Amsden cites James in his list of sources.

124. Kent, Kate Peck. **The Story of Navajo Weaving.** Phoenix, Ariz., Heard Museum of Anthropology and Primitive Art, 1962. 48p. illus. $2.00pa.

Illustrated with color photographs of blankets in the Heard Museum in Phoenix and also with a map and loom drawings, this is an excellent book on the Navajo rug. It is not a how-to-do-it book for weaving a rug, but it is an excellent guide to the art form. Ms. Kent covers the history, geography, loom drawings, and dye plants. No collection on weaving, particularly on the North American continent, should be without this informative, beautifully produced book. The low price of this book and Gilbert Maxwell's (entry 125) would make it possible to have both; there is some overlap but each has unique material that was carefully chosen. Another outstanding book for those interested in Navajo weaving is *The Navajo Blanket* by Mary Hunt Kahlenberg and Anthony Berlant (New York, Praeger, in conjunction with the Los Angeles Fine Arts Museum, 1973; 112p., illus.). This book contains excellent photographs of Navajo women weaving in the nineteenth century.

125. Maxwell, Gilbert S., and Eugene L. Conrotto. **Navajo Rugs: Past, Present, and Future.** Palm Desert, Calif., Best-West Publications, 1963. 72p. illus. $3.00pa.

Weavers, collectors, and anyone interested in Navajo rugs will want to see this book. For historical understanding, it is a must. There are many photographs of rugs, including 20 in full color, an excellent map of Navajo land showing rug weaving areas, and a detailed description of the types of rugs each area wove or now weaves. The author collected and dealt in Navajo rugs for 20 years before attempting this book. The result is a great success. Although there is a small section on how a rug is woven, it is not a how-to book. For a how-to book, see *Working with the Wool* (entry 119) by Noël Bennett and Tiana Bighorse, or Mary Pendleton's *Navajo and Hopi Weaving Techniques* (entry 126).

126. Pendleton, Mary. **Navajo and Hopi Weaving Techniques.** New York, Macmillan, 1974. 224p. illus. $9.95; $4.95pa.

Mary Pendleton has been working for years in her studio in Sedona, Arizona with Navajo and Hopi weavers and teachers. This clear, detailed treatment of their weaving art has emerged from those years of study. Rugs, sashes, and belts are covered, with 200 illustrations and a narrative so plain that even the beginner will be able to follow the instructions easily. Every technique is shown, along with alternatives to each. The techniques and the designs are authentic.

127. Reichard, Gladys A. **Navajo Shepherd and Weaver.** New York, J. J. Augustin, 1936; repr. Glorieta, N.M., Rio Grande Press, 1971. 222p. illus. $8.00.

A companion volume to *Spider Woman* (see below), this one deals mostly with spinning, dyeing, and weaving, touching on the Navajo culture as it pertains to those subjects. The photographs of each process are superb and are themselves a study of Navajo life. During the 1930s Ms. Reichard spent several summers with a weaving family on the reservation while she studied weaving. The step-by-step directions are well done, but the very beginning weaver will need to use Bennett's *Working with the Wool* (entry 119) or Pendleton's *Navajo and Hopi Weaving Techniques* (entry 126). No comparison between the books is implied, however, because Reichard is a total study and the other two make no pretense of being that. Dover Publications has just reprinted this book (1974; $3.00pa.). It is not an attractive publication— and it is certainly not on the level of the volume put out by Rio Grande Press.

128. Reichard, Gladys. **Spider Woman: A Story of Navajo Weavers and Chanters.** New York, Macmillan, 1934; repr. Glorieta, N.M., Rio Grande Press, 1968. 290p. illus. $8.00.

The title of this interesting, informative, and factual book comes from an old Navajo legend that begins "Spider woman instructed the Navajo women how to weave on a loom which spider man told them how to make." Ms. Reichard's works supplement each other; thus, the weaver will want to read both *Spider Woman* and *Navajo Shepherd and Weaver* (entry 127). Navajo culture is warmly presented here by a woman who lived with a family on the reservation in the 1930s. It discusses not only all aspects of weaving (sheep, spinning, dyes, weaving, and patterns) but also many of the ceremonies (such as a wedding). Anyone interested in Navajo weaving or in understanding a beautiful indigenous culture, will praise this book highly. Bibliography.

129. Wells, Oliver N. **Salish Weaving: Primitive and Modern, as Practiced by the Salish Indians of Southwest British Columbia.** Rev. ed. Cillivach, British Columbia, Salish Weavers, 1971. 36p. illus. $2.95pa.

Mr. Wells tells of Salish weavers through history and what they have woven. There are diagrams, photos of equipment and weavings, technical and how-to-do-it information, and a good section on Salish designs, plus a bibliography. Many of the photographs of blankets are in color. Mr. Wells has done a great service to the Salish in producing this book and an equally great service to weavers or those interested in North American weaving. The author has been instrumental in reviving interest in weaving among this particular Indian tribe and in obtaining outside recognition of their talents. It should be in libraries as well as in the private collections of interested individuals. Books such as Wells's *Salish Weaving*, Bennett's *Working with the Wool*, and Pendleton's *Navajo and Hopi Weaving Techniques* are contributions to culture as well as to weavers.

OFF-LOOM WEAVING
(Card, Inkle, Frame Loom, etc.)

130. Albaum, Charlet. **Eye of God.** New York, Grosset, in association with Parade Magazine, 1972. 87p. illus. $1.50pa.

An extremely useful and inexpensive book on the old folk art of creating beautiful pieces with various colored yarns. The beginner, craft teacher, and libraries will all find this an excellent source of information on this reviving art form. The author gives the history and development of the art and explains terms and materials. The illustrations, including the diagrams, are clear. There are directions for 19 complete projects, plus instructions (with diagrams) for basic weaves and variations, and for frames (from simple to complex).

131. Alexander, Marthann. **Simple Weaving.** New York, Taplinger, 1969. 112p. illus. $6.95; $3.75pa.

An introduction to building and weaving on various types of simple looms. Written with the needs of the beginner in mind, this book is a basic primer in the field. It contains 66 photographs that illustrate and supplement the text. The glossary and the suggestions on color harmony should be very useful to those who are just beginning to explore the delights of weaving. One of the best books for this level of weaving.

132. Alexander, Marthann. **Weaving on Cardboard: Simple Looms to Make and Use.** New York, Taplinger, 1972. 88p. photographs. $5.95.

Authored by an arts and crafts teacher, this book is directed toward the beginner. It shows how to construct and use 16 looms from such simple materials as soda straws and cardboard; the looms can produce useful items such as table mats, handbags, belts, and hangings. Good photographs supplement the explicit instructions and illustrate the use of color. This title, the author's other book, *Simple Weaving* (entry 131), and the film she made would comprise a very useful package of teaching materials for elementary school teachers, summer camp instructors, therapists, and others engaged in teaching creativity to young and old alike through simple weaving skills.

133. **Backstrap Weaving.** Minneapolis, Minn., University of Minnesota Agricultural Extension Division, n.d. 11p. illus. $0.35pa.

Clear black and white photographs and diagrams, plus a narrative, form an excellent guide to backstrap weaving. There is an introduction, a list of terms, a discussion of materials needed, and then instructions for making the heddle, making the backstrap, preparing the warp, threading the heddle, tying onto the beams, assembling the loom, and weaving. The novice will learn precisely how to do it. The Cooperative Extension Service, Kansas State University, Manhattan, Kansas, has published the same pamphlet (with full credit to the University of Minnesota) with a few added adaptations and illustrations. Also good is *Backstrap Weaving of Northern Ecuador* (Santa Cruz, Calif., Loom Books, 1974; 36p., illus.; $4.25pa.).

134. Barker, June. **Decorative Braiding and Weaving.** Newton Centre, Mass., Branford Co., 1973. 112p. illus. $7.50.

Black and white photos and diagrams illustrate the techniques for projects and finishing. The novice and the expert can benefit equally from the ideas presented here. The chapters include making simple cards, plaited braids, tablet woven braids, inkle loom braids, crochet braids, and hairpin crochet; there is also a chapter on textile construction. Jean Wilson's works (entries 169 and 170) will provide hints on finishing, as will West (entry 108) and others.

135. Bernstein, Marion H. **Off-Loom Weaving.** New York, Sterling, 1971. 48p. illus. $2.95.

A simple approach to weaving that uses equipment one would have around the house. There are 56 black and white and nine color illustrations (diagrams and photos) to supplement the narrative. Lampshades, feather capes, and dolls are among the projects. Craft teachers might get some ideas here.

136. Chamberlain, Marcia, and Candace Crockett. **Beyond Weaving**. New York, Watson-Guptill, 1974. 192p. illus. $14.95.

Here is an attractive survey covering fiber properties, felting, spinning, dyeing, single-element constructions, knotting, braiding and plaiting, wrapping and coil constructions, and card weaving. There are 28 illustrations in color and 250 in black and white. In addition to the how-to-do-it instructions, there are also ideas for projects. There is not much depth to the book but it gives a nice overview of many related crafts. Supplementary material includes a bibliography, a source list, and an index.

137. Crockett, Candace. **Card Weaving**. New York, Watson-Guptill, 1973. 144p. illus. $10.50.

Card weaving for every level of experience is treated exceptionally well here. History, materials, techniques, design, pattern drafts, double weave, and finishing are each given full treatment. A bibliography, index, and list of suppliers are also provided. The illustrations of completed works are absolutely beautiful; the picture of the cape made with strips sewn together will make the reader want to begin to card weave immediately. A superb book for libraries and individuals—for anyone who would lift card weaving from the ranks of the mundane.

138. Dendel, Esther Warner. **Needleweaving: Easy as Embroidery**. New York, Doubleday, 1973. 126p. illus. $7.95.

A nicely done book on needleweaving for those beginners who would like to work off the loom. The author shows what to weave and how. Wall hangings, tote bags, placemats, and handbags are among the projects. The illustrations are in color and black and white.

139. Droop, Joan. **Rugmaking**. Newton Centre, Mass., Branford, 1971. 65p. illus. $4.50.

The author, a teacher, a judge, and a demonstrator of rugmaking, has put together a good handbook on the subject including a brief history on the origin of rug weaving. Aimed at the novice, it provides detailed instructions and clear diagrams on types of stitches, stressing the importance of sound basic knowledge. Color is dealt with carefully, as are sources of design inspiration. Making a frame loom, dyeing yarn and simple weaving are fully explained.

140. **Foxfire**. New York, Anchor Books, 1973. $4.50.

Foxfire enthusiasts are many. *Foxfire 1* and *Foxfire 2* provide plans (good, bad, and indifferent) for making tools, etc., along with commentary by oldtimers. *Foxfire 2* has a section on weaving and spinning, with plans for wheels, spool racks, looms, shuttles, and more.

141. Groff, Russell E. **Card Weaving or Tablet Weaving.** McMinnville, Ore., Robin and Russ Handweavers, 1969. 47p. illus. $3.50pa.

These 53 patterns—each illustrated by black and white photographs, detailed diagrams, and detailed instructions—allow the beginner to weave immediately. Mr. Groff, publisher of *Warp and Weft* (entry 411) begins with a short history of card weaving, then explains how to make a card set if you can't find or don't want to buy one. Then he gives very careful directions that lead the novice to the actual weaving of one of the 53 patterns he has illustrated (belts, Christmas projects, and finishes for other projects such as handbag handles). Candace Crockett's *Card Weaving* (entry 137) would be the choice if one wanted to pursue the craft further.

142. Hoff, Anne. **A Simple Book of Belt Weaving.** Providence, R.I., East River Publisher, 1972. 24p. illus. $1.25pa.

A beginner's book (for child or adult) on inkle weaving; it includes directions for making an inkle loom. The price is low and the diagrams are plentiful (22 of them) and good. However, anyone even moderately interested in inkle will want to look at other titles in this section. They may be more expensive, but Atwater (entry 8), Holland (entry 143), and others provide much more detailed coverage than that attempted by Ms. Hoff.

143. Holland, Nina. **Inkle Loom Weaving.** New York, Watson Guptill, 1973. 144p. illus. $10.50.

This basic book will lead the novice step by step through inkle weaving. There is a good section on making your own inkle loom, plus some tips on how to sell your weaving. The instructions are supplemented by 242 black and white illustrations, plus 22 in color. Librarians, at least, will want to consider all the titles in this section on inkle weaving before spending $10.50 for this one.

144. Kelly, Karin. **Weaving.** With pictures by George Overlie. Minneapolis, Minn., Lerner Publ. Co., 1973. 32p. illus. (An Early Craft Book). $3.95.

Black and white drawings illustrate this dull book on weaving for children (primarily girl-children). It covers history, how cloth is made, making a cardboard loom, learning to weave, a wooden loom, and some projects such as a handbag, place mats, pot holders, and pillows. One face project is shown that might interest a very, very bored boy. With so many good weaving books available, why this one? Perhaps Wilson's *Weaving Is Fun!* (entry 170).

145. Kircher, Ursula. **Weaving on Kircher Looms.** Marburg, Germany, Kircher, 1970. 61p. illus. $1.95pa.

A well-written and nicely illustrated pamphlet, all in black and white, aimed at beginning weavers who have a small, table model tapestry loom. It would be of limited use to other weavers, since there are other books (Znamierowski, Beutlich, Wilson, etc.) that are more general and more useful, and that are in color.

146. Kliot, Jules, and Kaethe Kliot. **Card Weaving.** Berkeley, Calif., Some Place, 1973. 8p. illus. $0.75pa.

A leaflet on card weaving for the very beginner. The Kliots have also written a work on bobbin lace, available through Some Place; see entry 324.

147. Krevitsky, Nik, and Lois Ericson. **Shaped Weaving: Making Garments and Accessories with Simple Needle and Finger Weaving Techniques.** New York, Van Nostrand Reinhold, 1974. 120p. illus. $8.95; $4.95pa.

Two well-known craftsmen have collaborated on this fine book for both the beginner and the experienced. Collars, neckpieces, vests, sleeves, yokes, appliques, pockets, jewelry, bags, and hats are among the projects illustrated.

148. Kroncke, Grete. **Simple Weaving: Designs, Material, Technique.** New York, Van Nostrand Reinhold, 1973. 95p. illus. $5.50; $2.95pa.

The title aptly describes the book. It is well done, with clear, concise narrative and illustrations. There are projects for card, cigar box, cycle wheel, plank, rigid heddle, stretcher, and frame loom with heddles, and also projects using string. This book is for beginners, craft leaders, and others who would like a new idea or two. Ms. Kroncke's reputation for clearness and easy-to-follow directions is certainly upheld here.

149. McCall's Needlework and Crafts. **McCall's How to Weave It!** New York, McCall Pattern Co., 1969. 64p. illus. $1.00pa.

Excellent photographs accompanied by clear diagrams and careful directions make this a buy at $1.00. The projects are for the beginner using the following looms: frame, tapestry, backstrap, inkle, rigid heddle and table, four-harness. There is an index and buyer's directory. Make an afghan, picture, pillow, rug, wall hanging, bag, belt, necktie, poncho, ruana, scarf, stole, skirt, tunic, and (most impressive of all) toys. A lion, a llama, and two elephants (mother and baby) are alone worth the purchase price.

150. McCall's Needlework and Crafts. **McCall's Rugmaking.** New York, McCall Pattern Co., 1974. 64p. illus. $1.25pa.

Rya rugs by latch hook, woven rugs, punch needle rugs, and many more craft techniques are shown here. The photographs are most attractive and the diagrams and instructions are clear. It is for the beginner and for those who would create something lovely with a minimum of equipment. The woven rug chapter assumes one has a 27-inch, four-harness loom, or a tapestry or two-harness loom.

151. McCarthy, Nancy. **The Complete Guide to Rug Making.** New York, Drake Publishing Co., 1974. 192p. illus. $7.95. Announced for 1974.

152. Naumann, Rose, and Raymond Hull. **The Off-Loom Weaving Book.** New York, Scribner's, 1973. 190p. illus. $8.95.

The title (using the currently popular term for "primitive" or small loom) is not indicative of the contents, since the authors cover the frame loom, board, basket, Salish, tapestry, inkle, and card weaving—that is, both loom and non-loom. It is well done and would be of infinite help to craft teachers at all levels. Anyone could grow a bit by toying with some of the interesting and unusual ideas presented. The narrative and diagrams are very well done. The list of suppliers, however, is out of date.

153. Meilach, Dona Z. **Contemporary Leather.** Chicago, Regnery, 1972. 186p. illus. $10.00.

Another well-researched and well-written book by Ms. Meilach. The illustrations, 347 in black and white and 12 in color, are excellent. Aimed at the beginner, the book is a how-to explanation of techniques for leather, macramé, crochet, applique, clothing and weaving, batik, and tie-dye. Projects include pots, boxes, hats, and wall hangings.

154. Meilach, Dona Z. **Creating Art from Fibers and Fabrics.** Chicago, Regnery, 1973. 163p. illus. $8.95.

A "happening" in fibers and fabrics. The author creates imaginative works in crochet, wrapping, rug making, padded work, knotting, knitting, weaving, collage, patchwork, and more. The photographs of works are really the important thing in this book, which is rather a hodge-podge of creative ideas. There are instructions for some of the techniques (macramé, wrapping, sprang, and rug hooking). Suppliers of unusual fibers or fabrics or materials are noted.

155. Meilach, Dona Z., and Lee E. Snow. **Weaving Off-Loom.** Chicago, Regnery, 1973. 202p. illus. $12.95.

Another title by a major author in this craft; as usual, it is a good one. It is illustrated in black and white and covers weaving on frames, branches, cardboard shapes, and found objects. The author covers techniques of bobbin lace, knotless netting, crochet, knotting, and basketry. The book is expensive, but it's worth the money for those who are really interested in the author's techniques and in most of the material presented.

156. Miles, Vera. **Weaving Patterns for the Two-Way Loom.** Leicester, England, Dryad Press, n.d. 16p. illus. $1.00pa.

A handbook of pattern weaving on the rigid heddle or two-harness loom. Eight different warps are shown, with 44 distinctive patterns woven on them. Photographs of each weave, plus clear, brief instructions, present each pattern in such a way that a beginner can easily handle it.

157. Nilus Leclerc, Inc. **Cendrel No. 330, Métier Inkle Loom.** L'Isletville, Quebec, Nilus Leclerc, 1971. 18p. illus. $1.00pa.

Like most weaving equipment, the Leclerc Inkle Loom comes with directions on how to put it together and warp it, and gives some patterns. The booklet also tells one how to use the loom as a warping board.

158. Polkinghorne, R. K., and M. I. R. Polkinghorne. **Weaving and Other Pleasant Occupations.** New and rev. ed. New York, Bridgman Publishers, 1940; facsimile repr. Ann Arbor, Mich., Gryphon Books, 1971. 256p. illus. $12.95.

Why did Gryphon reprint this one? Dull black and white diagrams and illustrations supplement an exceedingly prosaic text; most of the information can be found elsewhere—and for less than $12.95. The book's aim is apparently to occupy children. The chapter headings include: tissue paper toys; picture and pattern making; materials for basketry; raffia-winding; plaiting with paper and raffia; weaving; spinning; cardboard looms for dolls' toys; weaving songs; etc. The sections on dolls' clothing, weaving songs, and dolls' furniture are the best ones in the book.

159. Rainey, Sarita R. **Weaving without a Loom.** Worcester, Mass., Davis Publications, 1966. 132p. illus. $8.95.

This book is for the novice of any age (from age three on up). It imaginatively explores simple weaving possibilities, using yarns, fabrics, fingers, cardboard, wire mesh, burlap, paper, straws, and materials from nature. Fully illustrated with 438 illustrations, 12 in color, the book emphasizes the creative approach and would be exciting to all weavers. The title is somewhat misleading; although some of the looms are simple, they are still looms. Regensteiner (entry 58) mentions this title in her bibliography, as do others. Rainey's other book, *Wall Hangings: Designing with Fabric and Thread* (Worcester, Mass., Davis Pub., 1971; illus. $9.95), could be a further source of ideas. The author is a devoted crafts person and her books are never a waste of time, for either beginner or expert.

160. Schulter, Lis. **Handweaving.** Denmark, CUM Textiles Industries, 1973. 68p. illus. $2.00pa.

This collection of projects for the CUM two-harness rigid heddle loom actually covers much more. Most of the projects form a basic course for beginners using this loom, with complete warping directions and other needed information. Also discussed are knitting directions for sweaters illustrated. For any weaver, however, the useful sections of the book are the metric conversion tables, yardages of CUM yarns, and helpful hints on amounts needed for projects.

161. Scorgie, Jean. **Warp and Weft of Weaving: Campus of the Air, 1973, 1974.** Corvallis, Ore., Oregon Educational and Public Broadcasting Service, 1973. 44p. illus. $3.00pa.

This is the text that accompanies the television course with the same title. The course itself was for two hours credit and was presented weekly (30-minute shows) on public TV in Oregon. The course will be repeated, and it certainly bears watching. The text, like the TV show, covers simple weaving on cardboard looms, homemade inkle and frame looms, cards, etc., using mainly items found in the home such as pencils and knitting yarn. Miss Scorgie has some clever ideas; those who want to learn simple weaving or those leading craft groups that don't have much money might find the TV program and/or the text to be an excellent source of information. More undertakings like this would be welcome.

162. Seagroatt, Margaret. **Rug Weaving for Beginners.** New York, Watson-Guptill, 1972. 104p. illus. $7.95.

All kinds of rugs—woven, inkle, tablet, on looms and off looms, hooked, braided, knitted and crocheted—are presented in this well-done book. Actually, it is more versatile than the title indicates; its interest will not be limited to beginners. In fact, one would have to be an extremely interested beginner to make the most of Seagroatt. Detailed instructions are given on how to design, sketch, draft, select colors and yarns, space, and measure. In addition, there are instructions for tie ups for warp looms, and information on the best types of yarn.

163. Snow, Marjorie, and William Snow. **Step-by-Step Tablet Weaving.** New York, Golden Press, 1973. 80p. illus. $2.50pa.

Another good craft book of the Step-by-Step series from Golden Press (Znamierowski, entry 115, is also part of this series). It presents the material with clear photographs, colored and black and white, and good diagrams. Altogether an excellent production at an excellent price, it will carry the beginner and also inform the experienced. For instance, the section on how to use cards to weave borders from fringe ends of a bag, etc., is very well done. Bibliography and supply list.

164. Sober, Marion Burr. **Eight Braids: For Belts, Trim, Bags.** Plymouth, Mich., Marion Burr Sober, 1972. n.p. illus. $1.25pa.

A small but impressive, inexpensive pamphlet by Sober that could be of use to many, including group instructors.

165. Specht, Sally, and Sandra Rawlings. **Creating with Card Weaving: A Simple Non-Loom Technique.** New York, Crown, 1972. 96p. illus. $4.95; $2.50pa.

This colorful, attractive beginner's book for cardweaving could easily be used by more experienced weavers as well. The how-to-do-it section is clear, but the most exciting part of the book consists of the photographs of the finished projects (such as wall hangings, articles of clothing, etc.). These stimulating ideas for card weaving have unlimited possibilities.

166. Tacker, Harold, and Sylvia Tacker. **Band Weaving: The Techniques, Looms and Uses for Woven Bands.** New York, Van Nostrand Reinhold, 1974. 104p. illus. $9.95.

With its 148 photographs, 49 line drawings, and a good narrative, this is a book that both the beginner and the expert can use to advantage. In addition to learning about techniques and looms, one can learn how to use woven bands in making scarves, ponchos, ruanas, pillows, rugs, chair pads, doormats, dolls, wind chimes, candleholders, and other items.

167. Turner, Alta R. **Finger Weaving: Indian Braiding.** New York, Sterling, 1973. 48p. illus. $2.95.

Summer craft teachers, elementary school art teachers, and home craftsmen should see this small, charming book on finger weaving. It illustrates numerous techniques for making beautiful North American Indian and ancient Peruvian designs (for instance, both lightning and double lightning). The directions are clear, and the equipment required makes the heart rejoice: six inches of pencil-sized dowel (or a pencil), a safety pin, and some bits of knitting worsted. Altogether a delightful book, with colorful photographs of the completed designs. It also has a bibliography, source of materials, and index.

168. **Weaving Techniques and Principles.** By the editors of Sunset Books. Menlo Park, Calif., Lane Books, 1974. 80p. illus. $1.95pa.

This introduction to weaving has the usual Sunset format and layout, with many color and black and white diagrams and illustrations. The contents, however, are not up to Sunset's usual standard and the book lacks the appeal it might have had. There are instructions on how to build and use a four-harness frame loom, along with some projects. Indexed.

169. Wilson, Jean. **Weaving Is for Anyone.** New York, Van Nostrand Reinhold, 1967. 144p. illus. $8.95.

Ms. Wilson's first book is as enchanting as her later ones. She introduces tapestry techniques and methods of weaving on small devices, with directions for making these looms (cardboard, frame, circle, and backstrap). The projects are well conceived and well illustrated. A good bibliography is included. Although any weaver can gain new insight from reading Ms. Wilson, the book is actually for the beginning weaver or the teacher of beginning weavers, and specifically for those working without a floor loom. Regensteiner (entry 58), Justema (entry 339), and many other bibliographies list Ms. Wilson's works.

170. Wilson, Jean. **Weaving Is Fun.** New York, Van Nostrand Reinhold, 1971. 140p. illus. $8.95.

The author's description, "a guide for teachers, children and beginning weavers, about yarn, baskets, cloth and tapestry," covers the contents very well. The book is *about* weaving; it is not a how-to book. It is, therefore, more suitable for the teacher than for the floor-loom weaver working at home. Ms. Wilson's *Weaving Is Creative* is a better buy for the serious floor loom weaver. Nevertheless, this one does contain an excellent chapter on fibers, yarn, and fabric. Appended are a glossary, a short annotated bibliography, and an index. Ms. Wilson, a renowned weaver and teacher of weaving, lives in Washington state.

171. Znamierowski, Nell. **Step-By-Step Rugmaking.** New York, Golden Press, 1972. 96p. illus. $2.95pa.

An inexpensive, well-written and well-illustrated book meant for the beginner. Like this designer-weaver's other books (see entry 115), this little work cannot be praised enough. It provides full discussions of embroidery, latch hook, crocheting, knitting, braiding, hooking, and weaving as used in making rugs (or in creating tapestries). Supplies, schools, books, periodicals, and book services are covered. The presentation of new designs and new ideas will stir the weaver's imagination.

TAPESTRY WEAVING

172. **The Art of Aubusson Tapestry.** Art Vivant, Inc., 173 Highbridge Road, New Rochelle, N.Y. 10804, 1972. 8p. illus. paper-folder type. free.

An excellent pamphlet prepared by the Tapisserie d'Aubusson to explain the Aubusson tapestry. Not a how-to book, however. Beautiful illustrations plus a well-done narrative make it a worthwhile addition to a weaver's library.

173. Beutlich, Tadek. **The Technique of Woven Tapestry.** New York,
   Watson Guptill, 1971. 128p. illus. $10.95.

A superb book by a well-known craftsman. Any weaver, at any level of
expertise, will find something of interest here. The section on building your
own tapestry loom is alone worth the price. However, there is a good deal more:
step-by-step instructions on how to weave a tapestry, weaving a sampler, how
to maintain an even width, tapestry and plain weave combined, warp and weft
face, and many other techniques. An invaluable guide and a marvelous book
for browsing.

174. Coffinet, Julien, and Maurice Pianzola. **Tapestry.** Geneva, Switzerland,
   Les Editions de Bonvent, 1971. 130p. illus. $9.75.

The ancient art of tapestry is beautifully presented in this unusually
well prepared book. The illustrations could not be improved upon and the
narrative supporting them is good. Historical development is covered in reproductions of lithographs that depict weavers and weaving, plus splendid color
reproductions of tapestries. The section on warping and weaving a tapestry
consists of a series of photographs that make the reader feel he is looking over
the shoulder of the weaver. Contemporary tapestry (to 1971), as interesting
as the rest, makes a fitting end to an exciting book. A chronological synopsis
of general history, history of the arts, and history of tapestry is followed by a
glossary and selected bibliography (in French). For a study of the purely
traditional tapestry, including techniques and how to build a loom, one would
choose Beutlich's *Technique of Woven Tapestry* (entry 173). And for
patterns, one would turn to Ingers' *Flemish Weaving* (entry 176).

175. Forman, W., B. Forman, and Ramses Wissa Wassef. **Tapestries from
   Egypt Woven by the Children of Harrania.** Rev. ed. Middlesex,
   England, Paul Hamlyn, 1968. 101p. illus. $15.95 (o.p.).

Although this book is at present out of print, it was revised and reprinted
in 1968 and may well be again; let us hope so, at any rate. The book presents
a collection of tapestries woven by children in a village in Egypt. The 66 color
plates are large and beautiful. The vitality, color, and imagination are
extraordinary. An exhibit of recent works from the village is presently tour-
ing the United States (1974). The exhibit is interesting, but it perhaps lacks
the spontaneity of the earlier works, since many of the weavers are no longer
children but have been weaving for some 20 years. Weavers will want to see
the book and the exhibit, if possible.

176. Ingers, Gertrud. **Flemish Weaving: A Guide to Tapestry Technique.**
   New York, Van Nostrand Reinhold, 1971. 112p. illus. $7.95.

A veritable joy for all tapestry weavers, would-be tapestry weavers, or anyone interested in the world of tapestry. An excellent chapter on the history of Flemish weaving in Sweden is followed by a discussion of weaving equipment, techniques, and materials needed. It would be worth seeing this book if only for the chapter on dyes and dyeing, which provides both historical and contemporary recipes. The patterns shown are old and new, simple and complex. In the back cover pocket are a number of full tapestry plans.

177. Jobé, Joseph. **Great Tapestries: The Web of History from the 12th to the 20th Century.** Tr. by Peggy R. Oberson. Switzerland, Edita S. A. Lausanne, 1965. 278p. illus. $35.00.

A superb book that is now out of print, although some bookstores and jobbers still have it. It is "coffee table" size, with many color photographs of the works discussed. The narratives have been written by known experts, as follows: "Gothic Tapestry" by Pierre Verlet (Cluny and the Louvre); "Classi cal Tapestry" by Michael Florisoone (Gobelins); "Contemporary Tapestry" by Adolf Hoffmeister (Prague); "The Weaver's Art" by François Tabard (Aubusson). Also included are prices of some tapestries sold at auction between 1960 and 1964, principal public collections, a bibliography, and an index. It is quite impossible to describe fully the scope and excellence of this beautiful book. For the continuing history of tapestry, one should see the review of *Beyond Craft: The Art Fabric*, by Mildred Constantine and Jack Lenor Larsen (entry 193).

178. Kaufman, Ruth. **The New American Tapestry.** New York, Van Nostrand Reinhold, 1968. 104p. illus. $13.50.

Many photographs of works by America's outstanding weavers along with a particularly interesting discussion of contemporary tapestries and woven structures make this an outstanding book. It is a record of avant-garde tapestries in the 1960s. Wilson (entry 170) proclaims it both useful and good, Justema (entry 339) says it is extraordinary, and Regensteiner (entry 58) also mentions it.

179. Kybalova, Ludmila. **Contemporary Tapestries from Czechoslovakia.** Tr. by Olga Kuthanová. London, England, Allan Wingate, 1963. 95p. illus. $5.95.

A good history and value judgment of the hand-woven tapestry in Czechoslovakia, written by the daughter of two distinguished tapestry artists. Modern weaving receives its full due here. This is a valuable book for all weavers who design their own creations and who need knowledge and stimulation from outside. Regensteiner (entry 58) lists it as a good source. The author has an interesting discussion of the problems of copying a painting for a weaving. There is a conclusion in English and a resume in French.

180. Rhodes, Mary. **Small Woven Tapestries.** Newton Centre, Mass., Branford, 1973. 144p. illus. $8.95.

The author, a teacher and weaver in England, has produced an excellent introductory book for weavers. Each technique is clearly explained, an historical background of tapestry is given, and then designing, weaving and finishing are discussed. Traditional and free-form tapestries are shown. The many illustrations are mostly black and white, although there are a few in color. Supplies are listed for Great Britain and the United States. Bibliography and index. This would be a good choice for a beginning weaver or a library.

TEXTILE HANDBOOKS

181. **American Fabrics Encyclopedia of Textiles.** By the Editorial Board of American Fabrics Magazine. Rev. ed. New York, Prentice Hall, 1972. 600p. illus. $39.95.

This is a major revision of the encyclopedia. It incorporates, among other major additions, the most recent developments in man-made fibers. This monumental volume covers all aspects of the history of textiles including carefully selected design ideas, the uses of fabrics, finishing fabrics, and the entire spectrum of natural and man-made fibers. Included in its 600 pages is a complete dictionary of textiles. For the serious weaver and those interested in the history and uses of textiles, this is an essential work.

182. Birrell, Verla. **The Textile Arts: A Handbook of Weaving, Braiding, Printing, and Other Textile Techniques.** New York, Harper, 1959; repr. New York, Schocker, 1973. 512p. illus. $7.95pa.

Ms. Birrell's work has been known for years as one of the definitive encyclopedic handbooks on textile arts. Znamierowski (entry 115) mentions it in her bibliography, as do most of the writers on textiles. Although it could be used as a how-to-do-it book, the handbook is actually a description of various methods and their histories. It is a good, detailed overview. The chapter headings are: fabric formation and design; history of weaving; textile fibers and yarns and their uses; simple looms and their uses; belt looms and belt weaves; rug looms and rug-making techniques; mechanically operated looms; basic weaves; non-woven fabrics; embroidery and needlework; dyes and dyeing process; textile painting process; textile stamping and printing process. There is a glossary, a bibliography, and an index. *Textile Arts* is a must for libraries and a welcome and basic addition to private collections. Other good books on textiles are: Adele Coulin Weibel, *Two Thousand Years of Textiles* (New York, Pantheon Books, 1952; repr. New York, Hacker, 1972; $60.00) and Isabel B. Wingate (ed.), *Fairchild's Dictionary of Textiles* (5th ed.; New York, Fairchild, 1967; $35.00).

183. Denny, Grace G. **Fabrics.** 8th ed. Philadelphia, J. B. Lippincott Co., 1962. 163p. illus. $6.95.

The eighth edition of the authoritative reference on fabrics covers all synthetics as well as transitional fabrics. First published in 1923, this handy tool lists technical and non-technical terms and fabrics alphabetically. Few people will want to buy one for the home library, but many will want to consult it at their local library.

184. Emery, Irene. **The Primary Structures of Fabrics: An Illustrated Classification.** Washington, Textile Museum, 1966. 339p. illus. $20.00.

Everything published by the Textile Museum is important, and this book is doubly so. It is the basic source and authority for any kind of textile. Each section has its own extended bibliography. Black and white photographs illustrate precisely what is meant. Part one deals with components of fabric structures, part two with classification of the structure of fabrics, and part three with structures that are accessory to fabrics. Every library need it for the reference collection, and every weaver will want to have it (or at least look at it).

185. Fisch, Arline. **Textile Techniques in Metal.** New York, Van Nostrand Reinhold (announced for Spring 1975). 128p. illus. $10.95.

The author shows how to use metal in weaving, knitting, crochet, braid, interlinking, sprang, bottin lace, and basketry techniques. Gold, silver, copper, pewter, and brass are discussed. The approach will stimulate many ideas.

186. Gale, Elizabeth. **From Fibers to Fabrics.** Rev. ed. London, Allman and Son, 1971. 230p. illus. $8.50.

The author, a lecturer in weaving at the London College of Furniture, has written a good book on the technical side of textiles. Yarns (natural and man-made), spinning and dyeing, weaving in general, weaving on the dobby and jacquard looms, plastics and non-woven fabrics, finishing, painting, care of fabrics, etc., are covered in this fine book. It is well illustrated. Recommended for the serious weaver and for libraries.

187. Leene, Jentina E., ed. **Textile Conservation.** Washington, Smithsonian Institution, 1972. 275p. illus. $15.00.

A basic knowledge of textiles and a little background in chemistry will suffice as background for this impressive book, even though the writing is highly technical. The book is the source for textile preservation and restoration. Among the subjects covered are natural dyes, textile cleaning, bleaching, textile pests, storage, display, and conservation. A "bible" for libraries and museums but also for your own shelf if you have a serious interest in textiles.

188. Pettit, Florence H. **America's Printed and Painted Fabrics**. New York, Hastings House, 1972. 256p. illus. $20.00.

Over 200 black and white illustrations (and six color plates) trace the carding, spinning, weaving, and the printing of fabric in America as it developed from its origins in England. This is an important textile book for the scholar.

189. Robinson, Stuart. **A History of Dyed Textiles**. London, Studio Vista, 1969. 112p. illus. $8.95.

A fabulous, scholarly, beautiful book to be read by everyone—not just by those with a particular interest in the subject. Excellent illustrations and knowledgeable text provide information on dyes, fibers, painted bark, batik, starch resist, discharge, tie-dye, and much more. One of the strongest parts of the book is the list of further sources for study. This is an excellent reference tool.

WEAVING WORLDWIDE, PAST AND PRESENT

190. Burnham, Dorothy K. **Cut My Cote**. Toronto, Royal Ontario Museum, 1973. 35p. illus. $2.00pa.

A gem of a book for libraries and individuals. No one will want to miss it. It is a study of primitive clothing, the materials of its construction (animal skin or loom), and how the materials determined its shape. The black and white illustrations are nothing less than perfect.

191. Channing, Marion L. **Textile Tools of Colonial Homes**. 2nd ed. Marion, Mass., Channing, 1971. 64p. illus. $2.25pa.

Ms. Channing describes her book as a study of textiles "from raw materials to finished garments before mass production in the factories." Walter E. Channing has prepared 62 excellent black and white drawings to supplement the interesting narrative. It would be difficult to imagine a weaver or spinner who would not enjoy and appreciate this attractively produced book. It will also be of use to libraries. The final chapter discusses the care and repair of old wheels and other equipment.

192. Clarke, Leslie J. **The Craftsman in Textiles**. London, G. Bell and Sons, 1968. 160p. illus. $6.95.

A book designed for the general student and reader in textiles, it includes: biographies of the field's great people of the past; warp and weft of weaving; ornament and design; weavers' tools and raw materials; dyeing and finishing; carpets; etc. There is a glossary and a bibliography. It would be useful as a general source in a library. It is a factual but not very exciting book.

193. Constantine, Mildred, and Jack Lenor Larsen. **Beyond Craft: The Art Fabric**. New York, Van Nostrand Reinhold, 1973. 294p. illus. $35.00.

Weavers, spinners, knotters, crocheters, knitters, stitchers, and other fabric producers must all delve into *Beyond Craft*. There are chapters on 18 artists, with large photographs (black and white and in color) of their work and of the artists at work, along with statements by each on his philosophy and method of producing. Some of the pieces may be more extremely contemporary than the reader is, but that is immaterial. This book is the most important statement yet to appear. The weavers run from Abakanowicz through Tawney to Weitzman in technique. It is a large, beautifully presented book, but many of the photographs do not do justice to the art pieces. A good introduction plus a bibliography and glossary add to the usefulness of this beautiful art book. Another work, more current, is *La Nouvelle Tapisserie* (text in French) by Andre Kuenzi (Geneva, Switzerland, Bonaventure, 1973; $50.00). It is handsome and very up to date; many of the tapestries were shown at the last Lausanne Biennial. A perfectly beautiful new book on *Sheila Hicks* and her weaving, written by Monique Levi-Straus, also gives a view of what's new in weaving. The book was published by Studio Vista in London, but Van Nostrand Reinhold are distributing it in the United States. It is $15.00.

194. Cordry, Donald, and Dorothy Cordry. **Mexican Indian Costumes**. Austin, Tex., University of Texas Press, 1968; 2nd printing, 1973. 373p. illus. $17.50.

With splendid photographs by Donald Cordry and a foreword by Miquel Covarrubias, this is, all in all, a handsome book. It is divided into two parts: part one consists of the general history of costumes, tools and techniques of making the pieces, the nature and variation of particular garments and accessories and how they are worn. Part two consists of an analysis of costumes from 27 villages. There are 276 black and white plates, and 16 in color. Today's handweaving often looks to Guatemala, Peru, and Mexico for inspiration. Consequently, weavers will want to see this book and, of course, libraries will want it for many reasons. Such cultural studies are important for studying the people of a country as well as their fabrics. A fine book on Japan is Tomoyuki Yamanobe's *Textiles: Arts and Crafts of Japan, Series No. 2* (English adaption by Lynn Katoh; Rutland, Vt., Tuttle, 1957).

195. CUM Textile Industries. **Scandinavian Handweaving and Rya**. Copenhagen, Denmark, CUM Textile Industries, 1974. 80p. illus. $5.95pa.

A new and attractive title by CUM Textile Industries, with a brief history of weaving and excellent photographs of ancient looms and weavings. The photographs of current ryas are also splendid and the instructions for weaving are clear.

196. Erdmann, Kurt. **Seven Hundred Years of Oriental Carpets**. Ed. by Hanna Erdmann and tr. by May H. Beattie and Hildegard Herzog. Berkeley, University of California Press, 1970. 238p. illus. $40.00.

Twenty color plates and 238 black and white photographs illustrate this handsome, scholarly book on rugs. It is one of the finest works on Oriental carpets. Those who have an interest in scholarly books on carpets (or other textiles, for that matter) should follow the book review section of the *Textile Museum Journal* (entry 409). The long, detailed reviews are written by experts.

197. Fisher, Leonard Everett. **The Weavers: Early American Craftsmen**. Illus. by the author. New York, Franklin Watts, 1966. 47p. illus. $3.95.

A perfectly lovely book with balanced, beautiful black and white drawings by the author. It is a very clear history and description of colonial weaving and spinning, designed for children (mostly grades 4 through 6) but suitable for young people or just about anyone. It contains no directions for weaving or spinning but provides, for its audience, the best descriptions available of wheel and loom parts and the weaving process. Plain weave, twill weave, summer and winter, and overshot are shown as patterns and drafts, and the flying shuttle is explained. Indexed.

198. **Handweavers Guild of America Slides Library**. West Hartford, Conn., Handweavers Guild of America, Inc., 1970.

These slide kits cover a variety of subjects pertaining to weaving, spinning, and dyeing. The kits have been assembled not only according to subject but also by age group. There are a few on special exhibits and conventions. The rental price, based on number of slides, ranges from $5.00 to $10.00; some kits are worth the price, some aren't. There are now available some slide/sound synchronized kits (one, for instance, is on Greek weaving).

Other useful shows for guilds are the exhibits that local guilds often prepare, which are available for mailing expense only. Such shows are advertised in *Shuttle, Spindle and Dye Pot* (entry 407). Some non-travelling, but very good, exhibits (such as the Nantucket School of Needlery [entry 251] exhibit library of natural dye samples) are available only if one visits the school.

199. Harcourt, Raoul d', and others, eds. **Textiles of Ancient Peru and Their Techniques.** Tr. by Sadie Brown. Seattle, University of Washington Press, 1962; 1st ed., Paris, 1934; repr. 1974. 329p. illus. $20.00; $8.95pa.

It is good to have this unusually beautiful and authoritative book on Peruvian textiles back in print. It describes and illustrates the intricate and varied techniques of pre-Columbian weaving, network, needlemade fabrics, and plaiting. It is the "bible" of ancient Peruvian textiles. This reprint has the complete text, all text figures, and all black and white photographs, although in a slightly reduced size.

200. Harrison, E. S. **Our Scottish District Checks.** Edinburgh, National Association of Scottish Woollen Manufacturers, 1968. 167p. illus. $15.00.

Scottish district checks are so named to distinguish them from the Scottish clan tartans. This fascinating account of district checks is also a history of Scotland. The only tartan to be included in the book is the Balmoral Tartan, of which a full account has been supplied by the Royal Family. The scholarship is meticulous, and the plates are not only accurate but beautifully presented. For those interested in the history of Scotland as well as for experienced weavers interested in the checks and plaids of that fascinating country.

201. Hesketh, Christian. **Tartans.** London, Octopus Books, 1972. 96p. illus. $5.95.

Weavers of tartans may well want to look at this book. It is a full history of the development and use of the tartan in Scotland. Beautiful color photographs, plus many in black and white (123 illustrations in all), show the history of tartans in fashion and their use among royalty, the army, and the clans. Libraries will be able to make good use of this title and also of these: Donald C. Stewart, *The Setts of the Scottish Tartans* (London, Oliver and Loyd, 1950), an outstanding work, now out of print; Sir Thomas Innis of Learney, *Tartans of the Clans and Families of Scotland* (Edinboro, A. K. Johnston, 1948; repr. 1964, with 114 color plates; $12.50); Frank Adams, *The Clans, Septs and Regiments of the Scottish Highlands* (Edinboro, Johnston, 1952); Robert Bain, *Clans and Tartans of Scotland* (Rev. ed.; London, Collins, 1968; $4.95), with handsome color photographs accompanying the history of each tartan.

202. Innes, R. A. **Non-European Looms in the Collections at Bankfield Museum.** Halifax, Bankfield Museum, 1959. 64p. illus. $2.00pa.

A real find for the weaver or scholar interested in non-European looms. The following are some of the African looms included: Ashanti narrow, Susu narrow, Mende tripod, Ewe narrow, Munshi narrow, Batta narrow, Egbo vertical, Igbo vertical mat, Cameroons vertical mat, Egyptian vertical and braid, Sudanese braid looms. Some of the Indian looms are the Bihar loom, Lahore rug loom, Agra braid loom. The Asian ones include Burmese frame loom, Chinese cotton, and Chinese sandal looms. The only Pacific loom is the Santa Cruz. There are explanations of how the looms worked, with drawings that show the loom, some heddles, and patterns. There are photographs of some of the looms. A glossary is included.

203. Kent, Kate P. **Introducing West African Cloth.** Denver, Colo., Denver Museum of Natural History, 1971. 85p. illus. $2.95pa.

This item was published in conjunction with an exhibition of African textiles at the Museum in 1971. It is meant to serve as an introduction to the subject. Nigeria and Ghana are the principal collection areas. The illustrations are black and white photographs of people working, cloth, looms, processes (such as dyeing), and drawings of designs used. In addition to the bibliography, there are four maps. It is an authoritative, well-done pamphlet that can easily stand alone. It is even more effective, however, when used with such a book as Roy Sieber's *African Textiles and Decorative Arts* (entry 213), also prepared to accompany an exhibit.

204. King, William A. **Warp and Weft from Tibet.** Repr. McMinnville, Ore., Robin and Russ Handweavers, n.d. 32p. illus. $3.50pa.

Fully illustrated with pen drawings (a diagram on each page), this is a guide to Tibetan rug weaving, including chapters on building the loom, (lap and floor), materials, the iron rod, the knot (as taught by Edith B. King), and an introduction and commentary by Earl L. King. An essential new work is *The Tibetan Carpet*, by Philip Denwood (Teddington H.O., Church Street, Warminster, England, Aris and Phillips, Ltd., 1974. 101p., illus. $30.00). This superb and scholarly book is copiously illustrated with photographs, both new and historical, of weavers and carpets.

205. Kybalova, Ludmila. **Coptic Textiles.** London, England, Paul Hamlyn, 1967. 157p. illus. $9.95.

More than 100 plates, with 62 in full color, detail these beautiful hand-woven fabrics. Ms. Kybalova has produced a definitive study of the Coptic textiles. It is not only an important, scholarly work, it is also a delight for browsers.

206. Ling Roth, H. **Ancient Egyptian and Greek Looms**. 2nd ed. Halifax, Bankfield Museum, 1951. 44p. illus. $1.95pa.

Black and white drawings of looms, warp weights, fabrics, combs, warp spacers, and tombs and museums bring ancient weaving to life. The Bankfield Museum has been the source of many pamphlets on textiles, for which weavers, spinners, and scholars are most grateful. Mr. Ling Roth also published *Studies in Primitive Looms* (3rd ed.; Halifax, Bankfield Museum, 1951).

207. Mead, Sidney M. **The Art of Taaniko Weaving**. Sydney, Australia, A. H. and A. W. Reed, 1972. 95p. illus. $3.75pa.

The Maori twining-finger technique using the native flax is well described in this book. The 34 black and white illustrations and over 100 diagrams will provide the craftsman working with fiber with new designs and techniques. Described by Wilson (entry 111) as "helpful and interesting." From the same publisher comes *The Art of Piupiu Making* (46p.; $3.95), an interesting book on making a Maori skirt.

208. Mitchell, Lillias. **The Wonderful Work of the Weaver**. Dublin, Ireland, Department of Education, 1972. 36p. illus. $1.75pa.

Not really a how-to book, the text ranges from types of sheep, varieties of spinning wheels, and lichen-dyeing recipes to a small section on weaving. The value of this book for reference collections will be the fact that it uses both Gaelic and English terms for weaving and spinning. The line drawings are attractive, and it would make a pleasant browsing book for those not already engaged in the crafts.

209. O'Neale, Lila. **Textiles of Highland Guatemala**. Washington, Carnegie Institution of Washington, 1945. 579p. illus. (Carnegie Institution of Washington Publication No. 567). $19.95.

Ms. O'Neale has given us the definitive guide to Guatemalan textiles. Yarns, looms, techniques for spinning and weaving, dyes and dyeing, textile design, and stitchery are covered in minute detail. Clothing of all kinds, including accessories, is discussed, with pattern layouts for many items. Handweavers with primitive to multi-harness looms will delight in this book. The text and illustrations abound with ideas.

210. Royal Ontario Museum. **Japanese Country Textiles**. Toronto, University of Toronto Press, 1965. 40p. illus. $1.00pa.

A catalog of the Royal Ontario Museum exhibition of Japanese country textiles. The booklet is printed in blue and white, which makes the illustrations quite attractive. An ancient loom is shown, along with many textiles—plain woven, single and double Ikat, and stenciled. The booklet is interesting by itself, without the exhibit, even though one loses much by not being able to view the textiles. Libraries and individuals interested in textiles should remember that museum exhibits and the excellent pamphlets or books published in conjunction with them are sources of information.

211. Seagroatt, Margaret. **Coptic Weaves: Notes on the Coptic Collection of the City of Liverpool Museum.** Liverpool, England, City of Liverpool Museum, 1965. 160p. illus. $2.50pa.

Truly a nice book on Coptic weaves; the author is a well-known weaver who understands the techniques very well and conveys them equally well. Black and white plates show the woven fabric; some are only a fragment of what the piece originally was. Yellow-page inserts show the minute diagrams of the patterns. The entire production has a good feel about it. It would take an experienced weaver to follow the diagrams, but anyone interested in fabrics will want to see the book.

212. Sherman, Vera. **Wall Hangings of Today.** Branford, England, Mills and Boon, 1972. 112p. illus. $11.50.

This work is divided into two sections, secular and ecclesiastical. The hangings shown were created by using the following art forms: batik, collage, embroidery, tapestry, tie-dye, and weaving. The photographs are good. There are some details of the actual creation of the hangings, and some mention of the artists' intentions. The hangings were selected from travelling exhibits that the author has prepared. There is a bibliography.

213. Sieber, Roy. **African Textiles and Decorative Arts.** New York, Museum of Modern Art; distr. New York Graphic Society, 1972. 244p. illus. $15.00; $7.75pa.

This splendid book on textiles and decorative arts surveys 26 African countries. The book was prepared to accompany the Museum of Modern Art's traveling exhibit of African Textiles and Decorative Art; it includes over 200 photographs from the exhibit and some from African history and life. Textiles are highlighted—woven cloth, beaten cloth, resist dye (beautiful tie-dye)—each more exciting in design and concept than the last. Every crafts person will want to see this outstanding work. No annotation could possibly describe the splendid and fascinating contents.

214. Stevens, Bernice A. **A Weavin' Woman.** Gatlinberg, Tenn., Buckhorn Press, 1971. 95p. illus. $2.25pa.

A little book on Clem Douglas, one of the people who worked toward saving the Southern Appalachian crafts from extinction. A book of love and faith, it can be enjoyed by all.

215. Thompson, Deborah. **Coptic Textiles in the Brooklyn Museum.** New York, Brooklyn Museum, 1971. illus. $11.00.

This useful and beautiful book is for the experienced weaver who needs inspiration or who just wants to know more about the art of weaving. As one might expect, the Brooklyn Museum has produced an excellent, scholarly work with great attention to detail. An introduction provides a general history of the subject, after which one or more pages illustrate the 40 individual textiles (in color) with a detailed description of each. A bibliography and comments are provided for each textile.

216. Tschebull, Raoul. **Kazak Carpets of the Caucasus.** The Near Eastern Art Research Center, Inc., 1971. 104p. illus. $9.50pa.

This beautiful catalog begins with a history of the particular type of weaving done where Turkey, Persia, and the Caucasus meet. The rugs are coarse and shaggy, with a limited number of designs and limited colors, all from natural dyes. The rugs differ mainly in their shades of color. The designs, handed down by rote from generation to generation, are mainly large, geometric medallions. The book consists largely of excellent reproductions of rugs, accompanied by a description and technical analysis. Historians, anthropologists, weavers, libraries—anyone interested in rugs will enjoy and value this book.

217. Victoria and Albert Museum. **Notes on Carpet-Knotting and Weaving.** By C. E. Tattersall. 2nd ed. Rev. by the Department of Textiles. London, Her Majesty's Stationery Office, 1969. 55p. illus. $1.00pa.

The author's object in this pamphlet is to detail hand-knotted and hand-woven carpet techniques used in Persia, Turkey, and other countries of the East. Photographs picture the finished product, while unusually clear plates illustrate the precise weaves and also the loom and its parts. The narrative, as one would expect, is a scholarly, historical study of carpets, design, and methods of weaving. Regensteiner (entry 58) and others draw attention to this in their bibliographies. It is an informative pamphlet for those interested in the subject.

218. Weir, Shelagh. **Spinning and Weaving in Palestine.** London, British Museum, 1970. 40p. illus. $1.50pa.

A good little book on the state of spinning and weaving in Palestine. The black and white photographs of the work in progress in homes and workshops show interesting aspects of the daily life of the people. The bibliography and glossary are useful. Not a how-to-do-it book.

219. Willcox, Donald J. **New Design in Weaving.** New York, Van Nostrand Reinhold, 1970. 123p. illus. $7.50.

This survey of weaving in Scandinavia at the present time is a critical evaluation of the craft, and not a how-to-do-it book. The only instructions in the book are two pages of rya knots. Willcox covers the geographical and craft areas thoroughly and concludes that weavers could well be more inventive. Materials for further study are appended, as well as a list of supply sources. This is a study that will interest weavers and non-weavers alike.

220. Wolf, Bernard. **The Little Weaver of Agato.** New York, Cowles, 1969. 48p. illus. $3.95.

A children's story of an Indian boy who lives in an Ecuadoran village in the Andes Mountains and who helps prepare the weaving that the family sells at the market. Excellent black and white photographs of the village and such activities as wool-gathering, spinning, and weaving. The photographs of the loom are particularly interesting. Now in any way a how-to-do-it book.

221. Zephyr Amir, M. F. **Supreme Persian Carpets.** Rutland, Vt., Tuttle, 1972. 138p. illus. $17.50.

Primarily a beautiful browsing book for carpet lovers, although it includes a brief section on knotting and weaving. Persian and Bokhara rugs have been photographed with great care, many in interior settings. For each carpet, there is a regional and historical description. Libraries and craftsmen will want this fine work.

SPINNING

222. Anderson, Beryl. **Creative Spinning, Weaving and Plant Dyeing.** New York, Arco Publishing Co., 1973. 60p. illus. $3.25pa.

An attractive paperback that the craftsman will find inadequate for several reasons. The author tries to cover too much material, with the result that spinning and dyeing are given only fair coverage and weaving is barely skimmed over. However, the non-craftsman might use the book to gain an elementary understanding of the processes. The excellent photographs could easily start someone on a new hobby.

223. Bankfield Museum Notes. **Handspinning in Egypt and the Sudan.** And **Hand Woolcombing.** By Grace M. Crowfoot and H. Ling Roth. Carlton, Bedford, England, Ruth Bean, 1974; repr. of Bankfield Museum's original pamphlets. 62p. illus. $4.25pa.

Ruth Bean has reprinted these two pamphlets as one book. The Bankfield Museum has done such excellent work on textiles that it would be a shame for the books to remain out of print. The title speaks for itself. The graphic illustrations are well done, as they usually are in the Museum's publications. Available from Ruth Bean, Victoria Farmhouse, Carlton, Bedford, England.

224. **British Sheep Breeds: Their Wool and Its Uses.** Middlesex, England, British Wool Marketing Board, 1973. 84p. illus. $3.95.

A history of growing sheep for wool, by R. Trow-Smith, is followed by material on 36 varieties of sheep. For each breed there is a full-page photograph (some in color) of a flock and a side-view close-up of an individual sheep; information provided includes a physical description of the sheep, where it is raised, classification and use of the wool, length of staple, fleece weight, and quality of the breed. This is an unusually interesting and well-done book that spinners and weavers will find fascinating. Libraries should also find it useful.

225. Castino, Ruth. **Spinning and Dyeing the Natural Way.** New York, Van Nostrand Reinhold, 1974. 100p. illus. $8.95.

This introduction to handspinning and natural dyeing begins at the beginning: shearing a sheep, plucking an angora rabbit, "fumphing" a silkworm cocoon, etc. There are 126 photographs, including four pages in color, by Marjorie Pickens. The text and the photographs together emphasize that spinning and dyeing are for everyone—adults and children. A field guide for dyeing is included.

226. Channing, Marion L. **The Magic of Spinning.** 2nd ed. Marion, Mass., Channings, 1971. 44p. illus. $1.50pa.

A charming and nicely produced how-to-do-it pamphlet on spinning. It includes a history of spinning and other germane facts (with an emphasis on wool). The fine, detailed drawings in the book are all done by Walter Channing. The book will be most useful for beginners, but others will also find it interesting. Appended are a list of interesting places for spinners to visit and a list of supply sources.

227. Chapin, Doloria M. **Let's Go Spinning: International Handspinning Directory and Handbook, 1971.** Fabius, N.Y., Thys'lldo, 1971. 91p. illus. $2.95pa.

Ms. Chapin's handbook is now out of print, but a new edition, price not yet set, has been announced for 1975. The booklet, which reflects a great deal of personal effort, is not only informative but very well thought out and well presented. It lists handspinners in both the United States and Canada, showing addresses, experience (novice through expert), the type of spinning that each does, whether or not they give lectures or demonstrations, and such miscellaneous information as whether they restore wheels and what to look for when buying one, preparing fibers for spinning, and other useful information.

228. Cox, Trudy. **Beginning Spinning**. Sydney, Australia, Wentworth Books, 1972. 39p. illus. price not available. pa.

Beginning spinning and dyeing are covered in this booklet, with easy-to-follow instructions. The author has written a serious, steady introduction to the craft, which also treats knitting with handspuns.

229. Craft/Midwest Magazine. **Spinning Sources List**. Comp. by Sherry Boemmel. Northbrook, Ill., Craft/Midwest, 1973. 7p. $1.00pa.

The list is rather comprehensive. However, those who receive the major periodicals in the weaving/spinning/dyeing field already have access to most of the sources through the classified advertisements. It is, as the title indicates, simply a list of source outlets for supplies. The description provided for each outlet is very general (wheels, repairs, natural dyes, mordants, etc.), with the price of the catalog or sample list noted. For a library or for a dedicated crafts-man it could save time. Arranged by supply source name only; no index.

230. Davenport, Elsie G. **Your Handspinning**. Pacific Grove, Calif., Select Books, 1953. 132p. illus. $4.25pa.

Like Ms. Davenport's books on weaving and dyeing, this one is the "bible" of its field. It covers wool sorting, wheels, flax, preparation, angora, plying of yarns, machine spun yarns, and much more. The black and white carefully made drawings are clear. The novice will use this book with profit and the experienced handspinner will also find it interesting. Index, bibliography. The fact that it has been reprinted many times since 1953 is a clear indication of its usefulness.

231. Duncan, Molly. **Creative Crafts with Wool and Flax**. Wellington, New Zealand, A. H. and A. W. Reed, 1971. 64p. illus. $4.25.

This book is a follow-up to the author's first book on spinning. It was planned as a pattern book to help spinners use natural fibers to the fullest extent. The chapters cover: planning threads; knitting with homespun wool; weaving with wool yarns; dealing with average and inferior wools; flax and its threads; color in our wool; and embroidery with wool and flax. It contains a source list and an index. A very interesting, attractive book that will most certainly be of interest to experienced spinners.

232. Duncan, Molly. **Spin, Dye and Weave Your Own Wool**. New York, Sterling, 1973. 72p. illus. $3.95.

Ms. Duncan provides a brief but well-illustrated survey. It ranges from selecting wool, preparing it, and spinning with a spindle and a wheel, to dyeing (including lichen), handweaving with an inkle loom (including plans for making one) and a frame loom, and even paddle warping a two-harness loom, plus a few patterns. Of course, in 72 pages it can answer only the simplest questions, but it is a good overview. It would be suitable for someone who wanted to begin reading about weaving, spinning, and dyeing. Appended are a supply list and an index.

233. Fannin, Allen. **Handspinning: Art and Technique.** New York, Van Nostrand Reinhold, 1970. 204p. illus. $12.50.

A monumental work by one of America's leading spinners and weavers. An exciting, important book to own because you will want to keep delving into it for information long after you have read it from cover to cover with fascination. For the beginner, as well as the expert; the section on yarn design alone would make it a worthwhile purchase. The text and illustrations are clear. A technical how-to book for scholarly spinners, it explains the "why" as well as the "how."

234. **Flax.** Dundee, Scotland, Flax Spinners and Manufacturers Association, 1971; also available: McMinnville, Ore., Robin and Russ Hand-weavers. $3.50 box.

A nicely done box that contains the following items: seed, root, stem, and blossom of the flax plant plus an illustration of same; samples of scrutch flax, hackled flax, grey and bleached yarn, flax twine plyed many sizes; a swatch of a belt made from flax; and swatches of both industrial and home materials made from flax. Very interesting for spinners, weavers, and those interested in fibers and fabrics.

235. Grasett, K. **Complete Guide to Hand Spinning.** Pacific Grove, Calif., Craft and Hobby, 1971; 1st English ed., 1930. 35p. illus. $1.85pa.

A good, well-illustrated paperback on teasing, carding, and spinning wool, flax, and silk with spindle and spinning wheel. It is by a well-known author and will be of use to beginners.

236. Kluger, Marilyn. **The Joy of Spinning.** New York, Simon and Schuster, 1971. 187p. illus. $6.75.

A personal, delightful book as casual as chatting with a friend—albeit, a very knowledgeable friend. Ms. Kluger tells of her experiences looking for spinning wheels and learning how to spin, plus a little family history. Wheels and their workings are described fully, as well as the preparation of a fleece and the methods of spinning the wool. There is a section on flax, although the author's main emphasis is on wool. Vegetable dyeing is also included. A book for the non-spinner but also for the novice or the experienced spinner.

It has a great deal of valuable information for all, and the author's comfortable style of writing makes this enjoyable reading.

237. Simmons, Paula. Reprints from *Handweaver and Craftsman Magazine* of ten articles by Paula Simmons.

Articles are on carding, spinning, overtwist, weaving with handspun, a three-part article on irregularity in handspun, and two articles on sheep raising for spinners. These combined for $1.80 (paper cover).

Also reprints from *Warp and Weft* on raising black lambs, spinning fine yarn, spinning heavy yarn, speed spinning, weaving handspun on a 100-inch wide loom. These combined for $1.30 (paper cover).

Available from Paula Simmons as well as from weaving and spinning supply outlets. Paula Simmons' well-deserved, fine reputation makes these reprints a good buy. Anyone, expert or novice, can get a tip, at least, from those excellent articles. Another find is a new and very well done book that will be of interest to spinners who raise their own sheep: Godfrey Bowen, *Wool Away: The Art and Technique of Shearing*, with an introduction by Allen Fannin (New York, Van Nostrand Reinhold, 1974; $4.50).

238. Spencer, Audrey. **Spinning and Weaving at Upper Canada Village.** Toronto, Ryerson (McGraw-Hill), 1964. 40p. illus. $1.50pa.

"Actually using the same tools and raw materials the pioneers had we attempt to produce similar materials." The museum community in the St. Lawrence Parks Commission, crafts section, is supervised by Ms. Spencer, and she writes about it well. The black and white photographs of rooms, equipment, textiles, and people at work are excellent. On the whole the pamphlet is most interesting and useful. A hearty thanks to the museums that give us such a splendid look at yesterday. Another charming picture of days gone by is M. Florence Mackley, *Handweaving in Cape Breton* (Sidney, Nova Scotia, Normaway Handicrafts, n.d.; $4.00). The author wanted to preserve the history around her, and she has succeeded. She has included history, a Gaelic weaving song, photographs and drafts of old patterns, pictures of old equipment, etc.

239. **Spinning Wool.** Richardson, Tex., Spincraft, 1973. kit. $13.00 boxed.

The spinning kit includes a drop spindle, rolags, cards, washed teased wool, instruction sheets, and a booklet "Spinning Wool" all for $12.00 (plus $1.00 postage). Spincraft also carries other spinning supplies and books.

240. **The Story of a Scottish Blackface Lamb.** London, British Wool Marketing Board, 1971. 58p. illus. $2.50.

Large, delightful, black and white photographs illustrate this narrative of a lamb from birth to two years of age. It is told by the lamb in first person. It is suitable for children although not actually a children's book. It would be useful for library collections.

241. Thomas, Sara Beth. **Angora Story: Bunnie to Bootie; A Handbook on Raising, Shearing and Spinning.** Carmel, Ind., American Rabbit Journal, 1967. 15p. illus. $1.50pa.

Ms. Thomas takes one to her immediate world to explain how to spin with Angora wool. She raises rabbits, shears them, and spins the wool using both the spindle and the spinning wheel. The pamphlet includes a good bibliography. (Many sources handle this pamphlet, including Gordon's Naturals in Roseburg, Oregon.)

242. Thompson, G. B., comp. **Spinning Wheels: The John Horner Collection at the Ulster Folk Museum.** Belfast, Northern Ireland, Ulster Museum, 1964. 52p. illus. $1.50pa.

Every library and every experienced spinner, as well as those people with only an historical interest, will want this pamphlet. An introduction to John Horner and the collection, a bit on the development of the spinning wheel, a classification and discussion of the equipment pictured is followed by 59 black and white drawings (many showing more than one piece). The drawings are beautifully done, and each has a gauge for measuring. It is impossible to recommend this pamphlet too highly.

243. Thresh, Christine. **Spinning with a Drop Spindle.** Santa Rosa, Calif., Threshold, 1971. 23p. illus. $1.00pa.

Spinning wool with a drop spindle, a method used for thousands of years, is the method used today by many peoples of the world (including the Navajo and Hopi in the American Southwest). The author of this booklet has excellent chapters on wool, washing wool, preparing clean wool for spinning, and spinning itself. The illustrations are pen and ink drawings that suit the subject well. This is a well diagrammed and clear introduction to drop spindle spinning; it is highly recommended for a beginner.

244. United States Department of Agriculture, Office of Information. Washington, D.C. 20250.

Bulletins are available for those who raise sheep, who are interested in raising sheep, or who are interested in fleeces. The following bulletins are illustrated and available for $0.25 each:

Bulletin No. 53: *Standards for Wool Top*
Bulletin No. 10: *Preparing Wool for Market*
Bulletin No. 135: *U.S. Official Standards for Grades of Wool*

Many excellent works are available through the government; most of them are listed in the *Monthly Catalog*.

245. Wool Education Center, Denver, Colorado.

WK-13: *Pressing, Blocking, Shaping* (4p.)
WK-56: *The Story of Wool* (25p.)
WK-58: *Wool Wisdom* (1p.)
WK-69: *Glossary of Wool Fabric Terms* (4p.)
WK-70: *Glossary of Wool Terms* (4p.)
WK-71: *Wool from Fleece to Fabric* (4p.)
K-19: *Grades of Wool and Sheep That Produce Them* (4p.)
K-20: *Breeds of Sheep, Photos of Sheep* (4p.)

Free unless you need more than 25 copies of each pamphlet, then $0.05 each. Good solid information.

DYEING

AND

RESIST DYEING

DYEING

246. Adrosko, Rita. **Natural Dyes and Home Dyeing.** New York, Dover,
1971; repr. of the 1960 ed. 154p. illus. $2.00pa.

Originally published as United States National Museum *Bulletin No. 281*
by the Smithsonian Institution Press. The first third of the book is devoted to
historical background and recipes from early books on dyeing, which makes it
interesting for the browser as well as for the serious dyer. The second part,
dealing with dye recipes, is a revision of Margaret Furry's work (entry 259).
The book contains over 150 recipes, both practical and historical, using
common trees, flowers, lichens, and weeds. In addition, there is a list of dye
plants and a list of colors, with the dyes needed to produce them. The instructions are clear and give variations; they also tell how to prepare material for
dyeing. The entire book makes fascinating reading. It is indexed and has a
good bibliography. Another title of great importance, just published, is *Nature's
Colors*, by Ida Grae (New York, Macmillan, 1974. 228p., illus. $14.95).

247. Bemis, Elijah. **The Dyer's Companion.** 3rd enl. ed. with a new introduction by Rita J. Adrosko. New York, Dover, 1973. 311p.
$3.00pa.

This is an unabridged reprint of the second (1815) edition. However, it
contains not only a new introduction, but also two appendices reprinted from
Natural Dyes and Home Dyeing by Rita Adrosko. The first edition of Bemis,
published in 1798, was the second known dye manual printed in the United
States. The introduction briefly presents what is known of his life and also
gives some hints on using the recipes. Dover has performed a real service in
reprinting this fascinating historical study. The home dyer will not find the
recipes functional as they stand, because they are in commercial amounts and
differing strengths. The Adrosko introduction covers the situation well.

248. Bolton, Eileen. **Lichens for Vegetable Dyeing.** London, Studio Vista
Publications, 1960; McMinnville, Ore., Robin and Russ Handweavers,
1972. 63p. illus. $4.95.

This is a necessary book for those who would dye with lichen. The
description of the plant, the history of its use for dyeing, how to gather and
prepare it, the various means of extracting the dyes and actually dyeing the
wool are all well treated and very usefully presented. However, it would be
extremely difficult to identify the lichen by the illustrations alone. Photographs of the various varieties of lichens closeup and in their natural settings
would have been much more useful. The one photograph in the book is of
lichen-dyed fleeces and it is excellent. A bibliography and index are included.
A new book, *Lichen Dyes of the United States*, by Phyllis Yacopino, is being
researched now.

For keying lichen, use the following book.

249. Hale, Mason E. **How to Know the Lichens.** Dubuque, Iowa, William
Brown, 1969. 226p. illus. $3.95pa.

For keying lichen to use for natural dyeing, this is a handy tool. Each
lichen is pictured against a map showing where it can be found. The book does
not, however, tell which ones give dye; for that one would use Bolton or
other books on natural dye sources.

250. Brooklyn Botanic Garden. **Dye Plants and Dyeing: A Handbook.** New
York, Brooklyn Botanic Garden, 1964. (A special printing of *Plants
and Gardens*, Vol. 20, No. 3). 101p. illus. $1.25pa.

Here is one of the "bibles" of dyeing, and rightly so. Because it is
fascinating, it is difficult to stop browsing long enough to write an annotation.
This pamphlet, with chapters by many authors, is for everyone—absolutely

everyone. It covers history of dyeing, ancient dyes, recipes, sources, plants from around the world, dyeing in Colonial New England, Aztec dye plants, a current Scottish garden of dye plants, workshops, historic bibliography, and much more. Every section is fascinating. If there is one fault, it is that the great Navajo and Southwest traditions of dyeing are not mentioned. Many of the seeds for dye plants mentioned here are available at Straw into Gold (see the list of suppliers, page 126).

251. Brooklyn Botanic Garden. **Natural Plant Dyeing: A Handbook**. New York, Brooklyn Botanic Garden, 1973. (A special printing of *Plants and Gardens*, Vol. 29, No. 2). 65p. illus. $1.50pa.

Another eagerly awaited dye book from the Botanic Garden, this one is just as fine as the previous issue. It covers color, dyeing with lichen, Navajo dyeing, Icelandic dyeing, dyeing with carrot tops, and a great deal more. Also included is a lovely folk tale about indigo. The Botanic Garden is preparing a film on plant dyeing, scheduled for spring of 1974. One of the articles is on natural dyeing at the Nantucket School of Needlery (Nantucket Island, Massachusetts). The school has a rare book library on dyeing, which scholars are allowed to use. The book includes a bibliography, supply source list, and index.

252. Bryan, Nonabah G., and Stella Young. **Navajo Native Dyes: Their Preparation and Use**. U.S. Department of Interior, Bureau of Indian Affairs, Indian Handcraft Series No. 2. Education Division, 1940. 76p. illus. $0.60pa.

Ms. Bryan, a Navajo, was an instructor in rug weaving at the Wingate, Arizona, Vocational High School at the time the study was done. The dyes described here are all found on the Navajo Reservation. Although she has dealt in the main with historical Navajo dyes, she has included a few of her own discoveries, such as the rose dye she obtained by fermenting the prickly pear cactus fruit. Line drawings illustrate the dye plants. The pamphlet is usually available from the Publications Service, Haskell Indian Junior College, Lawrence, Kansas 66044. In the spring of 1974 it was reported as out of print but being reprinted, though the date of reprinting was not indicated. This is one all dyers will want, and it is clear enough for the beginner. Another useful book, with a chapter on dyes and one on baskets, is *Indian Uses of Native Plants*, by Edith Van Allen Murphey (Mendocino County Historical Society, Calif., 1973; repr. of 1959 ed.; 81p., illus.; $2.50).

253. Colton, Mary, and Russell Ferrell. **Hopi Dyes**. Flagstaff, Ariz., The Museum of Northern Arizona Press, 1965. 87p. illus. o.p.

This is an important book that must be listed even though it is out of print. The recipes, which come directly from the Hopi, have been tested by the writer with the help of Hopi Indians. All instructions are given for dyeing cotton, wool, and baskets. It is a fascinating study of dyeing. One would not want to miss seeing a copy.

254. Conley, Emma. **Vegetable Dyeing.** 2nd ed., rev. by Meta Lewis. Penland, N.C., Penland School of Crafts, n.d. 35p. illus. $1.00pa.

A "bible" of dye books for the beginner and experienced person alike. Every dyeing collection should have a copy. This gem of a pamphlet is listed in almost every bibliography. The first edition was prepared in 1957/58, before Ms. Conley died in 1959, and the second a few years later by the woman to whom the first edition was dedicated. The recipes, which are clear, cover sumac berries, acorns, morning glory blossoms, etc., for a total of 31. There is room under each recipe for the dyer's notes. It should be noted that except for a small section on the actual dyeing process, the book consists only of recipes.

255. D'Angelo, Anne A., and Margaret B. Windeknecht. **Batik Handbook: A Color Guide to Procion Dyes.** Decatur, Ga., M. Windeknecht, 1972. 5p. swatches. $3.50pa.

Contains 46 swatches showing color strengths and mixtures of procion dyes, plus two pages of how-to-do-it. One would need to use another source for how-to-do-it batik (such as Ila Keller's *Batik: The Art and the Craft,* entry 287). However, having the color swatches certainly could be a convenience, since most dyers will not trouble to go through the elaborate laboratory tests to be this precise in the final color.

256. Davenport, Elsie G. **Your Yarn Dyeing.** Pacific Grove, Calif., Craft and Hobby, 1972– ; repr. of 1970 ed. 128p. illus. $4.25pa.

Natural and synthetic dyes and their applications are treated in detail here. Each process is discussed clearly and systematically. Wool, cotton, linen, silk, and synthetic fibers are all explained in how-to language. There is also an important chapter on color that will be helpful to those who have not previously studied color theory. If the beginning dyer is serious and intends to pursue the craft, this would be a good book; otherwise, it is more for the intermediate dyer. Like other books by this author, *Your Yarn Dyeing* is a classic in its field.

257. Davidson, Mary F. **The Dye Pot.** Rev. ed. Gatlinburg, Tenn., the Author, 1974. 53p. illus. $2.50pa.

Another of the "bibles" of dyeing, recently reprinted for the benefit of all who want to dye wool. The directions are clear and the explanations under each dye plant are excellent. The book was written after much experimenting by the author. There is a list of recipes by due material; except for a few of them, anyone can gather these materials. There is also a list of colors and the materials that produce them. She even includes plants that do not produce a good color or do not hold well—all of which makes this an exceptionally valuable book. Bibliography, index, and glossary.

258. Freeborn, Mary-Eleanor. **Dyeing for Beginners.** New Hope, Pa., The Loom Room, 1971. 8p. illus. $1.00pa.

Brief but clear and useful information on dyeing, for the beginner or the teacher of beginners. Ms. Freeborn is enthusiastic about her craft.

259. Furry, Margaret, and Bess M. Viemont. **Home Dyeing with Natural Dyes.** Washington, GPO, U.S. Department of Agriculture. Misc. Publication No. 230, 1935; repr. Santa Rosa, Calif., Threshold, 1973. 36p. $1.25pa.

Threshold has reprinted the Margaret Furry dyebook, which some will certainly want as an historical item. However, be advised that Rita Adrosko has included it, in full and revised, in her book, *Natural Dyes* (entry 246). Why pay $1.25 for the Threshold edition when one can get much, much more in Adrosko for $2.00?

The pamphlet was prepared because of a resurgence of interest in hand-crafts in 1935, and it has been basic to every dyer's library since then. The equipment section is well done, as is the discussion of steps to take. What one really cares about, of course, are the dye recipes—how many are there? The answer is that there are many, and they are varied and well explained. Beginners and experts can both use this book with ease. The lack of color charts is no problem; the descriptions are about as precise as one can be, especially since dyeing is different each time.

260. Gordon, Flo Ann. **Nature's Dyes.** Roseburg, Ore., F. Gordon, 1973. 13p. $1.00pa.

A nice little pamphlet on dyeing. Well written and printed, it is a good buy for the price. The author also puts out a "Natural Dye Pack" for $8.95 (postage included), which has eight different mordants; the *Nature's Dyes* pamphlet is included in the package, which contains enough mordant for at least five pounds of wool. Certainly a bargain for the beginning dyer. Ms. Gordon is well known for her teaching of natural dyeing.

261. Kramer, Jack. **Natural Dyes: Plants and Processes.** Drawings by Charles Hoeppner. New York, Scribner's, 1972. 144p. illus. $9.95.

There is good material here for the novice, the browser, or the experienced dyer. Excellent drawings of plants, a complete index, plus detailed recipes make this an exciting book. It covers gathering and processing plants and other dye material, preparing and washing wool, choosing and planting a dyer's garden, and sources for such a garden. Mr. Kramer urges the dyer to experiment. Altogether a most satisfactory book for dyers and libraries.

262. Kierstead, Sallie Pease. **Natural Dyes.** Boston, Mass., Branden Press, 1972. 104p. illus. $4.95pa.

A thoroughly enjoyable reading experience for those who dye, who want to dye, or who just want to browse through a book on natural dyeing. There are noteworthy descriptions of the dye plants and the historical background of many traditional dyestuffs, plus an alphabetical listing of the sources of dyes and the colors they achieve, and a partial list of dye plants arranged by colors. Dyes applicable for cotton, linen, silk, and wool are included, along with a good bibliography and an index.

263. Las Aranas Spinners and Weavers Guild. **Dyeing with Natural Materials.** Albuquerque, N.M., Las Pajaritas Studio, 1972. 23p. illus. $1.00pa.

A good buy at one dollar. This pamphlet has very informative, to-the-point instructions for preparing and dyeing wool; its good recipes cover such traditional dyes as madder and cochineal. Many of the recipes use plants native to New Mexico.

264. Leechman, Douglas. **Vegetable Dyes from North American Plants.** Toronto, South Ontario Unit of the Herb Society of America, 1968. 58p. $1.00pa.

This fine pamphlet on the use of natural dyes would be a good way for a beginner to start, but it will also be of interest to the experienced. It deals with wool only (and with wool that is already clean and ready to dye). The directions, which are perfectly clear, carefully lead the novice through the material he needs to know. A list of dye plants by color and a list of dye plants arranged alphabetically help one to the right recipes. Dyers think highly of this book. Indexed.

265. Lesch, Alma. **Vegetable Dyeing: One Hundred Fifty-One Recipes for Dyeing Yarns and Fabrics with Natural Materials.** New York, Watson Guptill, 1970. 114p. illus. $7.95.

The author, a professional teacher and consultant in textiles, has written an excellent text for the modern dyer. Vegetable dyeing, collecting, preserving the dye materials, equipment, and work space all are carefully looked into and presented in a practical fashion. Much interesting information touching on the perimeters of the subject is also given. An avid beginner could use this book, but it is mainly designed for the experienced dyer. Good color charts, bibliography, index, and sources of supply are also included.

266. Lloyd, Joyce. **Dyes from Plants of Australia and New Zealand: A Practical Guide for Craftworkers.** Wellington, New Zealand, A. H. and A. W. Reed, Ltd., 1971. 48p. illus. $3.95; $2.50pa.

An interesting book with addresses for firms in Australia, New Zealand, the United Kingdom, Canada, and the United States where ancient dyes can be purchased. The guide will probably appeal more to the exceptionally curious, experienced dyer—unless, of course, one lives "down under." However, there is no doubt that this is an excellent booklet with clear instructions, good photographs, and equally good drawings of plants. There are an index and a bibliography as well as dye sources.

267. Miranda, Catherine B., comp. **Natural Dyeing Notes.** Enl. ed. Preble, N.Y., Seven Valleys Weavers Guild, 1972. 35p. illus. $2.50pa.

Dye recipes and processes are well done in this pamphlet. The new section on lichen dyeing experiments is particularily interesting. It is, in the main, a compilation of dye recipes and results taken from other books, many of which are now out of print. In addition to the bibliography for the main body of the book, there is a separate one for the new section on lichen. The color index is also useful. Any dyer can benefit from this work.

268. Morrow, Mable, coordinator. **Magic in the Dye Pot.** Friendswood, Tex., C. F. Murray, 1966. 20p. illus. $1.60pa.

The dye recipes in this pamphlet resulted from a workshop in Santa Fe, New Mexico, in August 1966. The directions for using the 26 dye materials covered are explicit and the resultant colors are so clear that the lack of a color chart is no handicap. The dyes run from alder and red and white dahlia to madder, rabbit brush, etc. Although a beginner could use this book, some experience in dyeing would be helpful. Taggart, in her column in *Shuttle, Spindle and Dye-Pot*, lists it as a good source.

269. Pellew, Charles E. **Dyes and Dyeing.** New York, McBride, 1913. 259p. illus. o.p.

This is a former "bible" of dyeing. It contains much that is valuable for today's dyer, but it is also interesting as a historical source. Although it is out of print, most large public and university libraries will have a copy, and it is certainly worth searching for. Mr. Pellew covers history of dyes, modern dyestuffs, direct cotton or salt colors, theory and practice of color dyeing, the sulphur colors, indigo or vat dyes, basic and acid colors, dyeing feathers, leather and leather dyeing, silk and imitation silk, tie-dye, stencils and resist (including batik). It is a fascinating book.

270. Robertson, Seonaid. **Dyes from Plants.** New York, Van Nostrand Reinhold, 1973. 144p. illus. $8.95.

An absolutely superior dye book, this one will guide the rank beginner but will also capture the interest of the experienced. It is attractively presented with excellent layout, great color photographs, and clear black and white drawings. The chapters include preparing fibers, equipment for dyeing, mordants, gathering and using dye plants in every season, dyes of historical importance, top dyeing, lichen dyes, special dyes for cotton, linen, and silk, and planting a dye garden. There is also a section on putting the dyed threads and yarns to use in stitchery, weaving, knitting, crochet, knotting and plaiting, tie dyeing and warp dyeing. Contains a list of plants by dye color, an index of dye plants by common name, an index of plants by botanical name, and much more, such as a bibliography and a source list for suppliers. Everyone will want this excellent book.

271. **The Plictho of Gioanventura Rosetti: Instructions in the Art of the Dyers which Teach the Dyeing of Woolen Cloths, Linen, Cotton, and Silk by the Great Art as well as by the Common.** Tr. from the 1st ed. of 1548 by Sidney M. Edelstein and Hector C. Borghetty. Cambridge, Mass., MIT Press, 1969. 199p. illus. $27.50.

Even the paper in this beautiful, scholarly facsimile simulates the first edition. The complete Italian text and the original wood cuts have been reproduced, along with the translation and notes. It's even more exciting than Bemis' *Dyer's Companion*. Every dyer and scholar of dyeing will want to read Rosetti.

272. Ross, Nan. **Dyeing with Native Plants.** Illus. by Stuart Ross. Georgetown, Me., Sagadahoc Press, 1972. 23p. illus. $1.50pa.

A charming, little booklet printed by reproducing hand printing—black on grey. The pen-and-ink illustrations fit in well. The author's introduction covers materials needed, including chemicals, and gives a source. There is an explanation of how to prepare the cotton or wool for dyeing. Information given for each native plant includes mordant, timing, etc. The plants covered are wild lily-of-the-valley (or Canada may-flower), spruce bark, meadow sweet, alder, bayberry, huckleberry, interrupted fern. Note the price of Ross's book, and then check *Step-by-Step Spinning and Dyeing*, by Eunice Svinicki (New York, Golden Press, 1974. 64p. $2.95pa.). Although it is too recent to have been included as a separate entry, it is a super book that covers everything very well.

Smithsonian Institution Bulletin on Dyeing. See Adrosko, Rita.

273. Soderburg, Betty. **Color from Plants.** Hollywood, Calif., B. Soderburg, 1973. 16p. illus. $1.00pa.

A good bibliography and a lot of enthusiasm grace this little pamphlet on natural dyeing. The rest is just so-so, but the price is right.

274. Straw into Gold. **General Instructions on the Use of CIBA Dyes.** Oakland, Calif., Straw into Gold, 1971. 3p. $0.15.

Good, cheap instructions for the beginning home or class dyer using CIBA dyes on wool. The shop, Straw into Gold, not only sells the dyes and holds workshops but will help you by letter, if necessary.

275. Thresh, Robert, and Christine Thresh. **An Introduction to Natural Dyeing.** Santa Rosa, Calif., Threshold, 1972. 37p. illus. $1.50pa.

The Threshes have put together an attractive pamphlet on natural dyeing, with clear line drawings and excellent photographs. The explicit instructions can be followed by a beginner; the basic mordanting and dyeing processes have been reduced to nine steps. There are dye recipes using onion skins, marigolds, walnut hulls, oak galls, indigo, and others. An unusual and interesting photograph shows indigo "blooming." All dyers will want to see this booklet. Supply source and a color index are included.

276. Thursten, Violetta. **The Use of Vegetable Dyes.** Leicester, England, Dryad Press, 1972. 48p. illus. $1.75pa.

A collection of recipes that use natural materials to dye wool. There are sections on collecting, preparing, and storing materials; preparing dyebaths; mordanting; and scouring the wool. It is primarily for Great Britain, but it will also be of use in the United States. Among the 70 recipes are those for lichen, barks, foreign dyestuffs, and many types of natural dyes. Listed in the Brooklyn Botanical Garden bibliography and others, this booklet includes its own good bibliography.

U.S. Department of Agriculture. Pamphlet on Natural Dyes. See entry 259.

277. Worst, Edward F. **Dyes and Dyeing.** Pacific Grove, Calif., Craft and Hobby, 1970. 47p. illus. $1.50pa.

A reprint of the chapter on dyeing wools, from the old classic *Foot-Power Loom Weaving* (repr. Dover, 1974). It includes directions and formulae for using many natural materials. It will be of interest primarily to those who are making a serious, in-depth study of natural dyeing.

RESIST DYEING

278. Ash, Beryl, and Anthony Dyson. **Introducing Dyeing and Printing.** New York, Watson Guptill, 1970. illus. $7.95.

One of the publisher's "Introducing" series, obviously aimed at the beginner. There are step-by-step instructions for printing, dyeing, and decorating a wide range of materials. The major topics covered are relief methods, resist methods, discharge dyeing, stencil techniques, and recipes for dyes.

279. Bachem-Heinen, Tony. **Batik.** Tr. by Christian Albrecht. New York, McGraw-Hill, 1969. illus. $1.25pa.

A beginner's book on batik especially for grades four through six. It is one of the "Play Crafts" series.

280. Belfer, Nancy. **Designing in Batik and Tie-Dye.** Worcester, Mass., Davis Publications, 1973. 117p. illus. $9.95.

Basic technical knowledge is well presented here for several resist dye processes, including batik and tie-dye. A little history is included to make the beginner more knowledgeable and more comfortable in the craft. One of the author's stated aims is to encourage people to understand the art more fully and to bring tie-dye above the common. The sections on dyes and design are good and the photographs add to the appeal of the entire text.

281. Deyrup, Astrith. **The Complete Book of Tie-Dyeing.** New York, Lancer, 1972. 174p. illus. $1.95pa.

A good book, but for the beginner only. Covers equipment needed, basic steps, basic types of ties and techniques, fabrics and dyes, and seven elements of basic design. Projects are included, and there is a special chapter on tie-dyeing for children. A bibliography and a section on dye sources are included.

282. Deyrup, Astrith. **Getting Started in Batik.** New York, Bruce, 1972. 79p. illus. $2.95pa.

This is one of the Bruce series of books for beginners in crafts. Deyrup has done a particularly clear job of introducing batik, with a small section on tie-dye. Illustrations accompany the concise narrative, which begins with setting up the equipment and proceeds through sources of supplies. She has also included a section of helpful hints and definitions. Projects are included. The arrangement of the book makes it particularly easy to use for instruction. Projects include mobiles, a desk set, and an eyeglass case, among others.

283. **Dye-Craft.** Indianapolis, Ind., RIT, 1973. 26p. illus. $0.25pa. (to cover postage and handling).

Issued by the RIT Company, this is a guide to many forms of dyeing. It covers the ancient and contemporary dyeing skills of solid-dye, tie-dye, fold-dye, block-dye, pour-on-dye, and batik. There are suggestions for equipment, work area needed, and group sessions, plus many projects. Illustrations, diagrams, and color photos make this a nice pamphlet. For groups, the $0.25 cost will cover up to 10 copies. The address is Dye Craft, Educational Aids, Box 307, Coventry, Connecticut 06238. The pamphlet has merit; don't let its almost-free status or its promotional nature turn you away.

284. Hein, Gisela. **Printing Fabric by Hand: Beginning Techniques.** New York, Van Nostrand Reinhold, 1972. 79p. illus. $4.95.

First published in German in 1971, this is an excellent introduction for beginning students, teachers, and group leaders. It would be particularly useful for camp instructors and others who work with groups of various ages. Covers all sorts of materials suitable for making stamps (potatoes, cork, felt, clay, wood doweling, etc.), plus directions for finger painting. The projects have step-by-step directions.

285. Hobson, June. **Dyed and Printed Fabrics.** 3rd rev. ed. London, Dryad Press, 1967. 42p. illus. $2.95.

This introductory book for beginners covers batik, tie-dye, and block and screen printing on fabrics. Each method is described step by step; suitable for primary school students with or without adult help.

286. Hobson, June. **Batik Fabrics.** London, Dryad Press, 1972. 16p. illus. $1.70.

This introduction for beginners to wax resist dyeing describes the processes and includes detailed instructions for designing and creating in this traditional craft. The author has notes on the necessary materials and dyes, plus step-by-step instructions.

287. Keller, Ila. **Batik: The Art and Craft.** Rutland, Vt., Tuttle, 1966. 75p. illus. $5.25.

An exceptionally handsome book for the browser, the beginner, or the expert. It offers something for everyone. Well illustrated with photos, charts, and drawings, the text covers the history of batik and includes basic patterns, Indonesian batiks with ancient designs, modern batik methods, and examples of modern batiks. The step-by-step instructions should be perfectly clear to the beginner. Altogether it is a delightful book that will entice the reader to create a batik. Another title that must be noted for those who wish to go further into the subject is Alfred Bühler's *Ikat Batik Plangi* (Basel, Switzerland, Museum für Völkerkunde; 3v., 850p., illus.; $60.00). This work, with 506 black and white plates and 24 in color, covers resist dyeing, ancient and modern, in Asia, North Africa, Southeastern Europe. Text is in German.

288. Krevitsky, Nik. **Batik: Art and Craft.** Rev. ed. New York, Van Nostrand Reinhold, 1964. (Art Horizon Series). 92p. illus. $7.95.

The author, Director of Art for the Tucson Public Schools, is active in all fields of art and has exhibited throughout the United States. This good introduction to batik has clear and concise do-it-yourself instructions. The illustrations are particularly interesting, showing works by school children. Both the expert and the novice will be stimulated by this book. The possibilities of design seem endless. Another good work is Joanne Gibbs, *Batik Unlimited* (New York, Watson Guptill, 1974; 152p., illus.; $11.95). It has a clear, complete introduction, instructions for the beginner, and a bibliography and index.

289. Maile, Anne. **Tie and Dye: As a Present Day Craft.** Rev. ed. New York, Ballantine Books, 1969. 182p. illus. $6.50; $2.95pa.

A comprehensive book on the dye-resist process giving step-by-step instructions for beginners, hobbyists, students, or craft teachers. Special features are the section on methods of using tie-dye with small children and a "how-to" for kitchen dyeing. This good text is fully illustrated with diagrams, drawings, and color plates. Mentioned in Regensteiner (entry 58) as a source for color and design.

290. Maile, Anne. **Tie and Dye Made Easy.** New York, Taplinger, 1971. 160p. illus. $9.95.

Step-by-step instructions for beginners, including simplified methods and variations that could easily be used by those working with children or with any group where simplicity of approach is important. There is a good section on the selection of fabrics and dyes. The 370 color and black and white photographs and drawings supplement the text. All in all, it can be recommended for all who tie-dye or want to read about it. The author has included some ingenious thoughts and projects that make interesting reading for even the experienced tie-dyer. Deyrup (entry 281) mentions this book, as do others. It is a good choice for libraries and enthusiasts.

291. Martin, Beryl. **Batik for Beginners.** New York, Scribner's, 1971. 45p. illus. $4.95.

Here is a practical and historical introduction to this ancient art. The explanation of how-to-do-it for beginners is clear and simple. The historical section is particularly valuable, taking the beginner through the development of the art in Southeastern Asia.

292. Meilach, Dona Z. **Contemporary Batik and Tie-Dye**. New York, Crown, 1972. 224p. illus. $8.95; $4.95pa.

One of the publisher's "Arts and Crafts" series by a prolific, well-known craft writer. It is an introduction to both of these resist-dye methods, with nicely done illustrations. It has an index and a bibliography.

293. Mijer, Pieter. **Batiks and How to Make Them.**

A reprint of this 1919 book was announced by Finch Press (Ann Arbor, Mich.) for 1973; the reprint had not yet appeared at the time of publication.

294. Monk, Kathleen. **The Craft of Fabric Printing**. New York, Ballantine Books, 1969. 119p. illus. $2.95pa.

Formerly published by Taplinger under the title *Fun with Fabric*. The author prefaces the book with the following quote: "This is a practical book which has grown from helping students who are training to become teachers, many of whom wish to teach design through printing." Practically every technique of printing on fabric (adhesive, brush, tie-dye, wax, lino, etc.) is covered, with full step-by-step drawings and illustrations of the finished product. A well-done text for adult beginners, teachers, and group leaders.

295. Muehling, Ernst. **Book of Batik**. Rev. ed. New York, Taplinger, 1971. 72p. illus. $3.95.

The author carefully leads the beginner, step by step, through the creation of a batik. The book covers choice of material, tools, transferring the design, heating the wax, applying it, dyeing the material, and removing the wax, with clear descriptions and helpful photographs. All in all it is a very attractive book.

296. Néa, Sara. **Batik: Material, Techniques, Design**. New York, Van Nostrand Reinhold, 1972. 96p. illus. $5.50; $2.50pa.

Step-by-step instructions for creating a batik. The author shows the simple, complex, intricate, and beautiful fabrics that can be created by applying the process repeatedly to the same fabric. There are instructions for using a brush or a Tjanting tool as well as for batiking with blocks and stencils. The illustrations, both black and white and color, are good and supplement the text nicely.

297. Néa, Sara. **Tie-Dye: Designs, Materials, Technique.** New York, Van Nostrand Reinhold, 1971. 108p. illus. $2.95pa.

An excellent book for the serious tie-dye enthusiast. The book, originally published in Sweden in 1969, removes tie-dye from the level of the trite and elevates it to the level of an exciting art form. The illustrations, many in color, show precisely how the design will emerge, supporting the text well. The line drawings are particularly clear and graphic. A beginner or intermediate could use this book with excellent results, but the user must be truly interested in the craft and willing to take the time to turn out exceptional creations (for instance, an evening cloak is pictured in tie-dyed, unbleached poplin, with a silk lining).

298. Reis, Mary. **Batik.** Pictures by George Overlie. Minneapolis, Minn., Lerner, 1973. 31p. illus. $3.95.

This thin, colorful book is designed for children. It provides an introduction to batik and includes a few beginning projects.

299. Samuel, Evelyn. **Introducing Batik.** New York, Watson Guptill, 1969. 80p. illus. (Introducing Series). $7.95.

A beginner's book, as the title indicates. Instructions are complete for undertaking this resist-dye method, whether at home or at school. The 76 illustrations in 80 pages make this an exceptionally well-illustrated book. The narrative explanations are excellent. A special feature is the series of color photographs showing the dyebaths. Also, there are color photographs of many of the fabrics.

300. Shaw, Robin, and Jennifer Shaw. **Batik: New Look at an Ancient Art.** New York, Doubleday, 1974. 96p. illus. $3.95pa.

"Traditional motifs and creative new designs especially for the delicate art of batik, including 79 how-to illustrations with 12 full color photos, plus unique and exciting project ideas to batik yourself or use as inspiration for your imaginative designs" is the further subtitle of this good new book on batik. Although it was designed for the beginner, the experienced may also find some new ideas. The projects include simple doll, jointed doll, quilted doll, sausage-dog draft pillow, hobby-horse head, cushions, room dividers, lampshades, quilts, and costumes. Appended are a dye chart, a supply source list, and a bibliography. A good buy.

301. Stein, Vivian. **Batik as a Hobby.** Photos and illustrations by the author. New York, Sterling, 1969. 80p. illus. $3.95.

A fine introduction that could easily be used as a text for older children. The illustrations and text are very clear. Each chapter is devoted to one project, and the materials needed are clearly listed in the beginning paragraph. The projects, arranged in order of increasing difficulty, include placemats, a pillow, wall hangings, a lampshade, and a scarf. This would be an excellent book for learning the basic techniques. There is an index and a list of sources of supply. Another new, basic book is *Batik, Tie-Dye and Crayon Batik with Pull Out Design Section and Color Combination Charts* (Rosemead, Calif., Hazel Pearson Handicrafts, 1974; 34p., illus.; $1.50pa.). This pamphlet, designed for beginners, offers a lot of possibilities for learning the craft.

302. Strose, Susanne. **Potato Printing**. New York, Sterling, 1968. 48p. illus. $3.95.

Another of Sterling's "Little Craft Book" series, and an excellent one. It is a fascinating study of what can be accomplished in printing (or dyeing) a fabric or paper with a stamp made from a potato. Everything for the beginner or craft teacher is included here. The graded and well-illustrated projects, with step-by-step directions, are suitable for children as well as adults. Indexed.

RELATED CRAFTS AND OTHER ASPECTS OF WEAVING, SPINNING, AND DYEING

BASKETS

303. Angier, Bradford. **Wilderness Gear You Can Make Yourself.** New York, Collier-Macmillan, 1973. 115p. illus. $2.95pa.

This unusual work covers knots, braiding, baskets, and some dyeing, plus many other techniques required for this type of craft. Everyone interested in the make-it-yourself approach to outdoor life will be fascinated by this book. It can certainly be recommended as a very useful work for the beginner as well as for the more experienced.

304. Bobart, H. H. **Basketwork through the Ages.** Oxford University Press, 1936; repr. Detroit, Singing Tree Press, 1971. 174p. illus. $9.00.

Singing Tree Press (an imprint of Gale Research Company) has done the book world a favor by reprinting *Basketwork through the Ages*. This scholarly, exceptionally interesting history of basketry from earliest times is painstakingly footnoted, and the photographic reproductions are fascinating. Although it is not in any way meant to be a how-to-do-it book, it certainly will help the basket weaver understand the craft. Bibliography and index.

305. Cain, H. Thomas. **Pima Indian Baskets.** Phoenix, Ariz., Heard Museum, 196? 39p. illus. $1.25pa.

Mr. Cain, long-time curator of the Heard Museum, has prepared a scholarly work on the Pima basket. There are many photos, in color as well as black and white, to supplement the historical text. The book is still in print. Another title on Indian baskets, recently reprinted, is Carl Purdy's *Pomo Indian Baskets and Their Makers* (Ukiah, Calif., Mendocino County Historical Society; reprint of the 1900(?) ed. 44p., illus.; $1.50pa.).

306. Christopher, F. J. **Basketry.** Ed. by Marjorie O'Shaughnessy. New York, Dover, 1952. Unabridged and revised republication of W. & G. Foyle, 1951 ed. 111p. illus. $1.25pa.

One of man's oldest crafts, weaving baskets, is described in clear, simple language with equally clear illustrations. The basics that the beginner will need are well and fully presented, but the author goes so much further that the book will interest the experienced basket weaver as well. There are chapters on reed, willow, and coiled basketry as well as on raffia and rush work and the special problems of handles. The dyeing of reeds and raffia is covered also. Here are projects such as trays, stools, baskets of all kinds, and mats; there is information on finishing edges as well as on all kinds of stitching.

307. Cooke, Viva J., and Julia M. Sampley. **Palmetto Braiding and Weaving.** Miami, Fla., E. A. Seeman Publisher, 1947. 127p. illus. $5.95.

The designs illustrated here are simple but very beautiful, and the instructions are clear and concise. It would make an excellent book for the beginner in palm frond braiding and weaving. Because it includes so many projects, craft teachers and summer camp leaders should by all means see it. The authors have carefully studied the craft, and their account of the history and preparation of materials will be of interest to all craft people. Only one minor negative note intrudes: one wishes that the authors told how to dye the materials instead of simply saying that the dyes are expensive and that one can order fronds already dyed. Indexed.

308. Goodloe, William H. **Coconut Palm Frond Weaving.** Rutland, Vt., Tuttle, 1972. 132p. illus. $3.25pa.

Here is the book to have when you are shipwrecked on a tropical island, or, for that matter, when you are anywhere at all with a few hours to spare. A history of the coconut palm leads into excellent instructions, illustrations, designs, and techniques for weaving with the fronds. Hats, bowls, baskets, epergnes, long-handled leaf baskets, matting, decorations, and many other items are included. Instructions on how to cure the articles assures that the woven project will lead a long and useful life.

309. Harvey, Virginia I. **The Techniques of Basketry.** New York, Van Nostrand Reinhold, 1974. 128p. illus. $8.95.

Virginia Harvey, a name well known to craftsmen, has written an authoritative and excellent guide to basketry weaves including coiling, twining, wickerwork, splintwork, and plaiting, as well as variations in these. In addition to the clear narrative, there are 230 photographs (eight plates in color) and 229 line drawings to help the user.

310. Hiroa, Te Rangi (Peter H. Buck). **Arts and Crafts of Hawaii: Section 3, Plaiting.** Honolulu, Bernice P. Bishop Museum Press, 1964; repr. of 1957 ed. 41p. illus. $1.00pa.

This very scholarly work was written by the director of the Bishop Museum from 1936 to 1951. It includes an introduction, a discussion of materials, and an explanation of techniques for pandanus mats, sharp corners and interweaving, blunt corners, oplhl technique, fine pandanus mats, coarse sedge mats, makaloa mats and decoration, pillows, baskets, and fans. The illustrations include both drawings and photographs. The five-page bibliography, outstanding in itself, is for the entire series of 14 sections. Another interesting section of arts and crafts of Hawaii is *Twined Baskets* ($1.00pa.).

311. James, George Wharton. **Practical Basket Making.** New ed., enlarged and revised with new illustrations. 1917; facsimile reproduction, Seattle, Wash., Shorey Book Store, 1966. 125p. illus. $5.00pa.

The illustrations have suffered badly in this reproduction, but the text remains readable. Those who need only pointers or who are looking for a specific type of basket, weave, or stitch will find this work useful. For example, maiden hair fern basket, lazy stitch basket with a soft inner coil, the open Pima stitch and the Klikitat weave are all covered in detail.

312. Kroncke, Grete. **Weaving with Cane and Reed.** New York, Van Nostrand Reinhold, 1969. illus. $4.95.

Mentioned as a useful tool in *Weaving Is Fun*, this book seems to be a book to interest craft persons at all levels, except those already expert in this particular craft. The author presents and fully illustrates the materials and procedures for making attractive useful baskets.

313. Miles, Charles, and Pierre Bovis. **American Indian and Eskimo Basketry: A Key to Identification.** New York, Bonanza Books, 1969. 143p. illus. $2.98.

The authors have put together a beautiful book on basketry that will fascinate anyone interested in the subject and some who are not. The illustrations, in black and white, are mainly from the authors' collections. In addition to baskets, there are also pictures of other forms, such as a Nez Percé ration card, an Iroquois face mask, an Aleutian covered bottle, a Northeast California cap, a Northwest California cap, and a Klamath cap.

314. Navajo School of Indian Basketry. **Indian Basket Weaving.** Los Angeles, Whedon and Spring Co., 1903; repr. New York, Dover, 1971. 114p. illus. $1.75pa.

Dover reprints are usually bargains and this one is no exception. One hundred and fourteen illustrations (photographs and diagrams) supplement the narrative to give a how-to-do-it of many types of Indian basketry, such as Lazy Squaw, Mariposa, Taos, Samoan, Klikitat weaves, Shilo and Bam-Tsu-Wu baskets, shell weaving, beads and feathers, and the crossed warp twined weaving of the Indians of Washington state. And these are only a sampling of the many types covered. Anyone in the craft or anyone interested in a good academic study of basketry will want to see this book. The anthropological views expressed throughout could be looked upon as one historical view of the Indian or could be ignored altogether.

315. Perry, L. Day. **Seat Weaving.** 3rd ed. Peoria, Ill., Charles A. Bennett Co., 1952. 94p. illus. $2.00pa.

Everything you want and need to know about weaving seats of wood and cane, reed, rush or splints, is shown here. First published in 1917 by a manual training teacher and since revised, it gives step-by-step instructions. It was originally prepared for eighth grade boys. Certainly any beginner (or even the more experienced) will find excellent ideas for chairs, stools, flower holders, and other projects. Directions for finishing the items are also included. A special chapter on the "spider web" design has been added to this edition, for those already conversant with standard cane weaving.

316. Rossbach, Ed. **Baskets as Textile Art.** New York, Van Nostrand Reinhold, 1973. 199p. illus. $14.95.

Mr. Rossbach's book, sponsored by the American Crafts Council, is beautiful, scholarly, and very readable. It will be of great value to libraries and to those interested in either textiles or baskets. The illustrations (225 photographs, 15 line drawings, and 16 color illustrations) show how various types of baskets are made, and they also support the view of baskets as an art form. This superb book does great credit to its author.

317. Sober, Marion Burr. **Chair Seat Weaving for Antique Chairs.** Whitmore Lake, Mich., Michigan Graphic Corp., 1972. 64p. illus. $2.25pa.

This instruction book on weaving chair seats would be difficult to equal.
The directions, text, and diagrams are carefully prepared, with the beginner
in mind. The author covers caning, rush, splint and shaker weaves, plus more—
much more. Even the experienced antique chair seat weaver may find some
pointers here. A list of sources is included.

318. Tod, Osma Gallinger. **Earth Basketry.** Illus. by the author with an Intro-
     duction by Daniel Carter Beard. New York, Bonanza Books, 1972.
     169p. illus.

Basket weavers at all levels will enjoy this handbook. The how-to-do-it
instructions are concise, the diagrams are simple and clear. Photographs and
drawings accompany the text. It covers not only how to weave baskets but also
materials, such as runners, barks, splints, stems, vines, grasses, leaves, and
ferns. There are discussions of the form to which each material lends itself
most readily—round, flat, flexible, or novelty. The author also discusses the
states where particular plants and trees grow, telling where to find them and
how to prepare them. There is a list of supply sources and an index.

319. White, Mary. **How to Make Baskets.** New York, Doubleday, Page and
     Co., 1902; repr. Detroit, Gale Research, 1972. 194p. illus. $9.00.

Craft teachers for students of all ages will enjoy using this well illustrated book. The chapter headings reveal the contents: materials, preparation,
raffia, mats, simplest baskets, covers, handles, work baskets, candy baskets,
scrap baskets, bird's nests and oval baskets, finishing touches, how to cane
chairs and some Indian stitches. There is one delightful illustration of dolls'
furniture. The date of publication is an indication that the projects are not
of contemporary design, but all remain popular, at least.

320. White, Mary. **More Baskets and How to Make Them.** New York,
     Doubleday, Page and Co., 1912; repr. Detroit, Gale Research, 1972.
     157p. illus. $9.00.

A companion volume to Mary White's *How to Make Baskets*, this work
covers baskets (and techniques for making them) not considered in the previous
book. The drawings and instructions are as clear as in the earlier work, and the
entire book is very well thought out. A beginner in basket work can easily use
the book, but the more experienced will also enjoy it. It includes making basket centers and weaves, flower, practical, hanging, square, raffia and palm-
leaf baskets, as well as rush-seat chairs and palm-leaf hats. She also deals with
natural dyes and unusual materials. Included with the instructions for each
project is a list of materials and tools required for it.

BOBBIN LACE AND SPRANG

321. Andrews, Denison. **How to Make Your Own Hammock and Lie In It.**
New York, Workman Publishing Co., 1972. 96p. illus. $2.45pa.

A charming spiral paperback for fun-filled hours in making and using a hammock. The author gives a history, then writes about the Mayan hammock of Yucatan, the Twin Oaks type, the sprang method, and more. Finishing touches and final installation are also fully covered. A beginner can proceed nicely from the directions and the experienced will enjoy the variety presented in this excellent book.

322. Collingwood, Peter. **The Techniques of Sprang.** New York, Watson Guptill, 1974. 288p. illus. $25.00.

The meticulous research, writing, and diagramming that went into the author's well-known book on rugs is again evident in *The Techniques of Sprang.* It is a definitive guide to the finger-controlled method of braiding stretch threads to make stretch fabrics, a technique that has been in use for at least 3,500 years. Black and white illustrations (229 of them) supplement the text. There is a bibliography, an appendix, and an index. Novices, experts, teachers, and libraries will definitely want this important book.

323. Huetson, T. L. **Lace and Bobbins: A History and Collector's Guide.**
London, A. S. Barnes, 1973. 187p. illus. $6.95.

The author, a collector of bobbins, has written a fine scholarly work on English bobbin lace. A history of lace making in England, it includes many unusual facts that will be of interest to the serious student of bobbin lace. It is fully illustrated and has a bibliography and an index.

324. Kliot, Kaethe, and Jules Kliot. **Bobbin Lace: Form by the Twisting of Cords.** New York, Crown, 1973. n.p. illus. $7.95; $3.95pa.

A new look at a traditional textile art, written for the beginner and the expert alike. Four hundred and seventy-two photographs, 20 in color, illustrate the text. Also by Jules Kliot are *Sprang Language and Techniques* (1974; 16p., illus.; $1.50pa.) and *The Stitches of Bobbin Lace* (1973; $2.95pa.). The latter work is an analysis of how stitches are made and how they travel. Both of these titles are published by Some Place, Mr. Kliot's interesting and busy shop in Berkeley, California.

325. Maidment, Margaret. **A Manual of Hand-Made Bobbin Lace Work.**
McMinnville, Ore., Robin and Russ Handweavers, 1972. (Originally published in England by Isaac Pitman & Sons, 1931). 183p. illus. $12.50.

Lacemakers find this one of the most helpful tools for teaching traditional bobbin lace making. An introduction to the craft with materials used, general methods, various stitches plus different famous laces such as torchon lace, torchon corners, Cluny, Bedfordshire Maltese, Honiton lace, Buckinghamshire point ground, and others.

The following good books on lace making are distributed or have been reprinted by Robin and Russ Handweavers:

326. Gubser, Elsie. **Bobbin Lace.** $5.00.

Complete instructions including how to make your own pillow and bobbins with drawings and photographs, also 13 lessons on torchon lace, one on tape lace, and one on Brussells lace.

327. Mincoff, Elizabeth, and Margaret Marriage. **Pillow Lace: A Practical Handbook.** 231p. $12.50.

328. Tebbs, L. A. **The Art of Bobbin Lace.** 128p. $8.95.

Originally published in 1908, this book was intended for both beginners and advanced pupils. The full-size patterns are reprinted on two folding sheets. Ms. Tebbs was awarded a Gold Medal at the Franco British Exhibition in 1908.

329. Wright, Thomas. **The Romance of the Lace Pillow.** $11.50.

This is not an instruction book, but an outstanding history of the lace making industry in England from about 1500 to 1850.

330. Skowronski, Hella, and Mary Reddy. **Sprang: Thread Twisting, a Creative Textile Technique.** New York, Van Nostrand Reinhold, 1973. 96p. illus. $8.95.

The rebirth of sprang has led to increased inventive uses. This particular title provides an easy system of pattern direction and diagrams with hundreds of patterns. There are 104 photos, 78 line drawings, and four pages in color. Bags, pillows, skirts, vests, wall hangings, and more are discussed. The sprang enthusiast will also not want to miss Mr. Collingwood's *Techniques of Sprang* (entry 322).

331. Tod, Osma Gallinger. **Bobbin Lace Step by Step.** Coral Gables, Fla., the Author, n.d. 35p. illus. $3.50pa.

A simple, authoritative book on bobbin lace for the beginner. The author has also written many books and pamphlets on weaving, each of which is well done and authoritative. See the "Handweaving on Floor Looms" section.

COLOR AND DESIGN

332. Albers, Anni. **On Designing.** Middletown, Conn., Wesleyan University Press, 1943. 81p. illus. $4.95pa.

There are a few black and white illustrations, but the book is mainly a discussion of design and weaving. Ms. Albers goes into some detail on design and weaving at the Bauhaus and then discusses designing weaves in general. The author is an authority and her book is important. Ms. Albers' husband, Josef Albers, has written an excellent book for the weaver who wants to understand more about color—*Interaction of Color* (abridged ed.; New Haven, Conn., Yale University Press, 1971; $8.50). This work originally appeared in 1963.

333. Bager, Bertel. **Nature as Designer: A Botanical Art Study.** New York, Van Nostrand Reinhold, 1973. 196p. illus. $15.95.

Excellent black and white studies. A great book that every weaver, rug hooker, and fabric designer will want to study. The author uses black and white photographs taken from nature (flowers in bloom, leaves, plant stems, etc.) to show not only their own beauty of design but also their possible use in designing. It is an exciting book for all who would use their eyes as more sensitive instruments for a fuller enjoyment of life.

334. Bothwell, Dorr, and Marly Frey. **Notan: The Dark-Light Principle of Design.** New York, Van Nostrand Reinhold, 1968. 79p. illus. $6.95.

Notan, an excellent exercise for creative design, goes beyond most books in showing and explaining emotion in design. The black and white illustrations used throughout to enhance the narrative are well conceived, and the concepts are further supported by photographs of gates, snowflakes, glassware, and more. Anyone, beginner or expert, could obtain valuable ideas from *Notan.* Another good title is *Introducing Design Techniques,* by Robert Capon (New York, Watson Guptill, 1973; 96p.; $7.95).

335. Encisco, Jorge. **Design Motifs of Ancient Mexico.** New York, Dover, 1953. 153p. illus. $2.50pa.

An unabridged, unaltered copy of the first edition, published in 1947. Here is an unusually rich source for design ideas for every craftsman. There are 766 vigorous, primitive designs, including geometric, natural forms (birds, dogs, flowers, etc.), the human body, and artificial forms (twists, braids, etc.). The material is copyright-free and 10 items may be incorporated for any single use without fee or special permission. A jewel of a find for design. The black and white illustrations are so clear that they could be traced. Rug hookers and weavers will find it useful.

Also excellent are: Le Roy H. Appleton, *Indian Art of the Americas* (New York, Scribner's, 1950; 279p.; repr. New York, Dover, under the title *American Indian Design and Decoration*; $4.00); Bill Hohn, *Northwest Coast Indian Art: An Analysis of Form* (University of Washington Press, 1965; 115p.; repr. $4.95pa.); and another book by Jorge Encisco, *Designs from Pre-Columbian Mexico* (New York, Dover, 1974; 104p.; $1.50pa.; 300 illus.); or for a more modern approach, see Mickey Klor Marks, *Op-Tricks: Creating Kinetic Art*, with kinetics by Edith Alberts (New York, Lippincott, 1972; 40p., illus.; $1.95pa.).

336. **Greek Ornament.** Tr. and intro. by Patrick Connell. New York, Dover, 1968. 127p. illus. $4.95.

Presented here are 800 illustrations of Greek ornament as a source for design. Some of the illustrations are black and white drawings, while others are photographs. It would be an excellent reference tool for the public or private library. All levels of ability should find it stimulating to the imagination.

337. Guyler, Vivian Varney. **Design in Nature.** Worcester, Mass., Davis Publications, 1970. 124p. illus. $9.95.

These 124 black and white photographs of nature (leaves, flowers, etc.) make an inspirational book for weavers. It is form, composition, and art. A book to see.

338. Itten, Johannes. **The Art of Color.** New York, Van Nostrand Reinhold, 1973. 155p. illus. $40.00.

A handsome book by an expert, covering the subjective experience and rationale of color. It will be of use only to those who wish to delve deeply into the question of color, but to such people it is essential.

Other excellent titles on color include Faber Birren, *Creative Color: A Dynamic Approach for Artists and Designers* (New York, Van Nostrand Reinhold, 1961; 128p.; $15.00); and *Goethe's Color Theory* by Johann Wolfgang von Goethe, arranged and edited by Rupprecht Matthaei, translated and edited by Herb Aach (New York, Van Nostrand Reinhold, 1971; 275p.; $27.00); and *Theory of Colors* by Johann Wolfgang von Goethe (Cambridge, Mass., MIT Press, 1973; 488p.; $12.00; $2.95pa.). Among other titles noted in Regensteiner (entry 58) or Znamierowski (entry 115) are M. Chevreul, *The Principles of Harmony and Contrast of Colors and Their Application to the Arts* (New York, Van Nostrand Reinhold, 1967; 256p.; $30.00); Patricia Sloan, *Color: Basic Principles and New Directions* (New York, Van Nostrand Reinhold, 1968; $2.75pa.); and Charles N. Smith, *Student Handbook of Color* (New York, Van Nostrand Reinhold, 1965; 95p.; $7.95).

339. Justema, William, and Doris Justema. **Weaving and Needlecraft Color Course**. New York, Van Nostrand Reinhold, 1971. 160p. illus. $9.95.

A book to read, consult, or browse in—but above all, to see. The basis of the text is the alternate title ("color course; a handbook for weavers and needlecraftsmen who use colored materials that, on being mixed together, do not undergo physical change"). There are 50 special projects to do, and six threading drafts and tie-ups are shown for the more compilcated ones. A good bibliography, glossary, and index accompany the book. An indispensable tool for all libraries and individuals whether beginning, intermediate, or advanced.

340. Klein, Bernat. **Eye for Color**. London, Collins, 1965. 136p. illus. $9.95.

Mr. Klein, a textile designer who operates his own company, has produced a handsomely laid-out book with color plates (some of which are his own paintings, with fabrics designed on the basis of the paintings). It is biography, philosophy, and experience put together in a great package. In total, it is his view of color, textiles, and what can make the world a grand place to live in. This is an impressive, thoughtful effort that should be read by everyone interested in textiles—and also by those just interested in color, clothes, or life around them.

341. **String, Raffia, and Material**. New York, Franklin Watts, 1970. 183p. illus. $5.95.

An intriguing book that helps young children create at their own level. It will stimulate their own projects as well as show them how to do the ones in the book. Useful in starting children in three-dimensional design as well as flat design. Projects, which use various types of materials such as string, raffia, and wool, are described and graded by level of difficulty. Each shows the materials needed, illustrates the steps, and shows the final product (such things as plaiting bells, woven mats, a hippopotamus, dolls, a glove puppet, and cushions). Craft teachers should relish this book. It is very colorful. Indexed.

342. Ward, Michael. **Art and Design in Textiles**. New York, Van Nostrand Reinhold, 1973. 112p. illus. $8.95.

Color, light, aspects of design, how to form ideas, and more in a good book on design in textiles. The 61 photographs (including 12 in color) and the 49 line drawings are good. This is a needed book that should be of great use to libraries as well as to textile craftsmen.

MACRAMÉ

343. Ackerman, Lejeune Whitney. **Macramé: A New Look at an Ancient Art.** Sunnyvale, Calif., Lejuene, 1973. 64p. illus. $2.50pa.

This book (one of a craft series) promotes the use of Lejuene swistraw ribbon in macramé. For the beginner or the crafts teacher, it has instructions for projects, supplemented by black and white and color photographs of completed projects.

344. Andes, Eugene. **Practical Macramé.** New York, Van Nostrand Reinhold, 1971. 118p. illus. $3.95pa.

A handsomely illustrated introduction to macramé aimed at those beginners who would like to become proficient enough to try out original ideas. There may well be ideas here for the more experienced. This work is one of those mentioned by Laura Torbet as being well done, which is in itself a good recommendation. Gene Andes, a semi-retired physician, works with his wife Ellen, a semi-retired librarian, who is responsible for many of the pieces of macramé in the book. One of their articles on three-dimensional macramé appeared in *Handweaver and Craftsman* (May/June 1972). Their book, *Far Beyond the Fringe*, was published in 1973. Some of the projects in this book are for belts, purses, a bikini, and vests, and there is a discussion of ways to use leather in macramé. There is a list of suppliers.

345. Andes, Eugene. **Far Beyond the Fringe: Three-Dimensional Knotting Techniques Using Macramé and Nautical Ropework.** New York, Van Nostrand Reinhold, 1973. 160p. illus. $9.95; $4.95pa.

A book for the advanced macramé enthusiast and for libraries, but also for those who might be interested if they could carry the craft beyond the usual. The photographs and illustrations are excellent and the techniques are clearly described. Since most of the projects suggested are large, the author has included some practical hints on how to handle and store the supplies (mostly rope). He makes the projects look worthwhile and fun.

346. Barnes, Charles, and David P. Blake, in collaboration with William Baker. **Macramé Fashions and Furnishings.** Great Neck, N.Y., Hearthside Press, 1972. 256p. illus. $8.95.

A lively and imaginative publication that proceeds from the introductory stages to material that is quite advanced. The illustrations, 14 in color and 63 in black and white, are particularly interesting. Projects include hangings for bells, lamps, containers, a bracelet, eyeglass case, and Christmas tree. Indexed.

347. Bress, Helene. **The Macramé Book**. New York, Scribner's, 1972. 274p. illus. $12.50.

If only one macramé book is to be bought, buy this one; it is one of the most useful published so far. Lively and comprehensive, it will be useful to beginners and experienced macramé enthusiasts, and also to weavers who would combine macramé and weaving. Among the book's unique features are a chart of knots, table of yarn sizes, charts of cords per inch, and an indication of the length of cord needed for various projects. The illustrations, many in color, are exceptionally well done and the diagrams are particularly graphic. A list of suppliers is included.

348. Close, Eunice. **Macramé Made Easy**. New York, Collier Macmillan, 1973. 88p. illus. $3.50.

Here is a step-by-step guide for the beginner in macramé; for many of the projects, the guide suggests an unusual approach using soft materials. A shawl, a macramé lace collar, an evening bag, and a bed jacket are a few of the projects given. The illustrations, in color and black and white, are good. The techniques shown are quite basic and the projects are not as wild as those found in Andes' *Far Beyond the Fringe*. Indexed.

349. Dépas, Spencer. **Macramé, Weaving and Tapestry: Art in Fiber**. New York, Macmillan, 1973. 144p. illus. $8.95.

The textile arts are presented here in a modestly priced, well-done guidebook for the beginner. The photographs, diagrams, illustrations of projects, and narrative are clear, ranging in coverage from basics to combinations to original design. He discusses dyeing (both cords and yarn), and double weave is also covered. A list of suppliers is included. An excellent book for libraries, novices, craft teachers, etc.

350. Graumont, Raoul. **Encyclopedia of Knots and Fancy Rope Work**. 4th ed. Cambridge, Md., Cornell Maritime Press, 1970. 690p. illus. $15.00.

A leading nautical author has compiled a complete text that is designed for the sailor but that will delight the macramé enthusiast as well. The experienced knotter will use this encyclopedia to discover fascinating new ways of creating macramé. Step-by-step instructions are given for each of the 3,668 knots shown. Arrangement of the book is from the simplest knot to the most complicated. Both text and drawings are used to help the reader.

351. Graumont, Raoul. **Handbook of Knots**. Cambridge, Md., Cornell Maritime Press, 1945. 197p. illus. $2.00pa.

Four hundred twenty-eight knots are shown, and there are 47 plates. The book deals with all kinds of knots, not square knots alone. The experienced macramé enthusiast will use it as a source of new ideas; as the title indicates, no projects are included. Torbet (entry 373) and others include this in their bibliographies.

352. Graumont, Raoul, and Elmer Wenstrom. **Square Knotting or Macramé: Square Knot Handicraft Guide.** Cambridge, Md., Cornell Maritime Press, 1949; repr. New York, Random House, 1972. 212p. illus. $3.95pa.

A guide for beginners (and for experts who might have forgotten a knot or two). The book has easy-to-follow directions, with excellent illustrations and little text. Diagrams and photographs help the novice achieve the desired knot. Well done, as are all the Graumont books. Listed in the bibliographies of Ms. Regensteiner (entry 58) and others

353. Harvey, Virginia. **Color and Design in Macramé.** New York, Van Nostrand Reinhold, 1972. 104p. illus. $7.95.

A worthy follow-up to the author's *Macramé*, published in 1967. Although it gives a good review of knots, this text will probably be best for the macramé enthusiast who has already mastered some basic techniques. Color and design are presented in detail with particularly interesting comments about "add-ons" such as pebbles, beads, etc. There is an exciting section on the knotted form as a three-dimensional study useful for sculpture. And color, color everywhere. It is an excellent book.

354. Harvey, Virginia. **Macramé: The Art of Creative Knotting.** New York, Van Nostrand Reinhold, 1967. 129p. illus. $3.95pa.

The author explains and describes many variations and uses of macramé that will interest other craftsmen as well as the macramé enthusiast. Torbet (entry 373) feels that this is one of the best and most comprehensive texts published; it is also mentioned in Wilson, Regensteiner, and most selected bibliographies on the subject. It is a delightful book and should probably be a first purchase. The author packs instructions, projects, tools, ideas, history, list of suppliers, bibliography, and glossary into an exciting package.

355. Holdgate, Charles. **Net Making.** Drawings by the author, photographs by Alec David. New York, Emerson Books, 1972. 136p. illus. $5.95.

Step-by-step instruction, illustrated by line drawings, makes this a perfect book for the group leader, the beginner, or the experienced craftsman who needs a quick refresher. Indeed, there are projects here for everyone: basketball carrier, a two-color shopping bag, a hammock, a crab pot, and many more. There are also separate chapters on finishing, further projects, and knots.

356. LaBarge, Lura. **Do Your Own Thing with Macramé**. New York, Watson Guptill, 1973. 150p. illus. $11.95.

The author, a professional craftsperson, has not written a how-to-do-it manual, but has tried to lead the reader to use his own imagination in planning projects. There are diagrams, black and white illustrations, and some color photographs of the author's own works. A well-written, well-conceived book that will serve libraries as well as the true macramé craftsman.

357. La Croix, Grethe. **Beads Plus Macramé**. New York, Sterling, 1969. 49p. illus. (Little Craft Book). $2.95; $0.95pa.

Macramé and embroidery with beads are the subjects of this "Little Craft Book" from Sterling Press. Belts, covered bottles, jewelry, and other projects help the novice learn to apply the knotting technique to beadcraft. Craft teachers and young people will find ideas of interest. The illustrations are in color and black and white.

358. Lily Mills. **Macramé: The Captivating Art of Decorative Knotting**. With directions by Jan Orr. Shelby, N.C., Lily Mills, n.d. 4p. illus. $0.25 leaflet.

An excellent leaflet of instructions for macramé, printed on four legal-size sheets. This would make a nice starting point for macramé group instruction.

359. **Macramé: Creative Knot-Tying**. By the editors of Sunset Books and Sunset Magazine. Ed. by Susan Lampton. Menlo Park, Calif., Lane Books, 1972. 80p. illus. $1.95pa.

An introduction to macramé for beginners only. The illustrations and text are clear. Not indexed. Other titles are perhaps more suitable for the serious beginner in macramé (Torbet, Harvey, Meilach, for example). However, this one is well done, nicely designed (as one expects the Sunset books to be), and inexpensive.

360. **Macramé Hangups**. Rosemead, Calif., Craft Course Publishers, 1973. 23p. $1.00pa.

A delightful pamphlet on creating macramé hangers for plants, lights, wind bells, etc. The color photographs showing how to use the "hangups" inside and outside are great. For all levels.

361. Marein, Shirley. **Off the Loom: Creating with Fibre.** New York, Studio Viking, 1973. 96p. illus. $8.95.

A potpourri of good information (not all off-the-loom, as the title would have you believe) presented in a manner suitable for the beginner. The sections cover techniques of braiding, wrap twining and wrapping, knotting, macramé, natural dyeing, and many other topics, with clear directions for finishing the projects. Some of the illustrations are in color. The author's emphasis is on experimentation and discovery. There is a bibliography and an index.

362. McCall's Needlework and Crafts. **McCall's Book of Handicrafts.** New York, McCall Pattern Co., 1974. 224p. illus. $8.95.

Among the many instructions for handicrafts designed for the beginner are the following: batik (hangings, fashions, ties, and bags); macramé (belts, bags, necklaces, rings, hangings, bottle covers, and pillow); tie-dye (ties and scarves); weaving without a loom (wall plaques, hangings, potholders); weaving on a small loom (sampler hangings, belts, pillows). This catch-all of crafts for the beginner, the library, or the teacher has 110 attractive illustrations, 68 in color; the instructions are detailed.

363. Meilach, Dona Z. **Macramé: Creative Design in Knotting.** New York, Crown, 1970. 212p. illus. $7.95; $3.95pa.

An excellent book for the beginner, though the more experienced may also get some ideas from it. It is clear, fully illustrated, and easily followed. Finished works by other artists are shown to give the reader hints on finishing. Torbet (entry 373) calls it "one of the best and most comprehensive published." In October 1971, *Craft Horizons* reported that 20,000 hardcover and 80,000 paperback copies had been sold.

364. Meilach, Dona Z. **Macramé Accessories: Patterns and Ideas for Knotting Clothing, Handbags, Jewelry, Household Items.** New York, Crown, 1972. 96p. illus. $4.95; $2.50pa.

A popular author for popular crafts. Here is a wealth of material, including specific patterns, projects, and ideas, with complete directions for each. The book also provides beginners with instruction in the basic knots, and there is a review for the more experienced. Many tricks of the trade are discussed, such as adding cords, making picots, and wrapping. Excellent photographs illustrate the text for such projects as belts, bags, hats, vests, necklaces, sandals, hammocks, plant hangers, and placemats.

365. Paulin, Lynn. **Macramé**. Rosemead, Calif., Hazel Pearson Handicrafts, 1971. 32p. illus. $1.50pa.

This is an easy-to-follow, illustrated (black and white and color) guide for teachers and hobbyists. It includes basic instructions plus patterns for 21 macramé projects (wall hangings, purses, necklaces, mats, belts, etc.). Nice. Inexpensive.

366. Pesch, Imelda Manalo. **Macramé: Creative Knotting**. New York, Sterling, 1970. 48p. illus. $2.95.

This excellent, step-by-step text covers creative knotting, braiding, and twisting; threads, cords, and yarns; and basic tools, aids, and materials needed to begin. Clear and numerous illustrations make this work (one of the "Little Craft Book" series from Sterling) a good choice for the beginner. Teachers could use this as a text for older children or for groups of any age. The projects included are fine for beginners and well laid out.

367. Phillips, Mary Walker. **Step-by-Step Macramé**. New York, Golden Press, 1970. 80p. illus. $2.50pa.

Craft Horizons (October 1971) reports that this book has sold 700,000 copies—and with good reason. The Golden Step-by-Step series is excellent throughout. Considering the price and the contents, this is a bargain that no enthusiast should overlook. Photographs (color and black and white) plus diagrams lead the beginner and the more experienced to the creation of hanging planters, tote bags, room dividers, patio hangings, bracelets, and much more. Includes a bibliography and a supply list.

368. Short, Eirian. **Introducing Macramé**. New York, Watson Guptill, 1970. 96p. $7.95.

A fine book for the beginner in macramé, it has 84 photos, with four pages in color and 34 line drawings. Materials, equipment, and techniques are discussed, and then projects such as fringes, braids, fabrics, garments, and accessories. Torbet (entry 373) lists Short in her bibliography.

369. Smith, Hervey Garrett. **The Marlinsplice Sailor**. Tuckahoe, N.Y., John De Graff, Inc., 1972. 131p. illus. $7.95.

Here is a great source for new knots and new rope materials. Although aimed at the nautical market, it will also be of interest to serious students of macramé.

370. **Square Knot Booklet, No. 1.** 11th ed. Brooklyn, Herwig, 1970. 30p. illus. $0.75pa.

This booklet, first published by Herwig in 1926, has gone through many editions. The square knot, explained and illustrated with photographs, is shown in many forms; there is information on how to begin and finish knotted projects in several different designs, plus directions for making six different belts. Macramé enthusiasts will be interested in this. Advertisements are included. The sequel to this booklet is *Square Knot Booklet, No. 2*, which gives more advanced designs, instructions for making five handbags, and directions for more difficult knots (e.g., Turk's head and double carrick bend).

371. **Square Knot Booklet, No. 3.** 4th ed. Brooklyn, Herwig, 1970. 83p. illus. $1.75pa.

This is the "Square Knot" series pamphlet that will interest macramé creators. It is a combination of the first two, with the addition of instructions for making different handbags, a square knot centerpiece, and a square knot tie. Black and white photographs plus clear diagrams illustrate the techniques. Advertisements are included. Although it lacks the vivid color, attractive layout, and high-fashion ideas of macramé books such as those by Andes, Torbet, Meilach, etc., this pamphlet is interesting in its own way.

372. Strom, Nils, and Anders Enestrom. **Big Knot Macramé.** New York, Sterling, 1971. 48p. illus. $2.95.

For the beginning macramé enthusiast (and particularly for men), here are large and bold creations. The projects, which use large cords, are for sturdy items such as rail covers and mats, with directions also for hitching a bottle cover. First published in Sweden, this well-done introduction was written by two men who teach knotting to sailors. Not only are the step-by-step instructions clear and profusely illustrated, but also the section on finishing projects is good. It is one of Sterling's "Little Craft Book" series.

373. Torbet, Laura. **Macramé You Can Wear.** New York, Ballantine Books, 1972. 115p. illus. $3.95pa.

Laura Torbet is a successful designer and now an equally successful author. "A complete basic course in macramé and 25 brand-new wearable projects with full instructions," the subtitle of this book, is an excellent description of the contents. The fully illustrated instructions are clear, and projects range from beginners' knotting through fancy beading, lacing, and pendants. If one pays attention to the directions, it is almost impossible to make a mistake. A bibliography and buyer's guide are included.

374. **Vogue Guide to Macramé**. New York, Stein and Day, 1973. 80p. illus. $6.95.

Definitely a Vogue quality production geared toward women, this is a good introduction to the subject. In addition to a short history of the craft, it covers equipment and materials, setting on threads, knots, etc. The black and white illustrations are clear. It tells one how to start and finish, work in the round, wash, dye, and much more. Projects include an apron, a shawl, a pinafore, a poncho, sundry bags, a lampshade, and a table mat, among others. It would be a good choice for the novice.

375. Walker, Louise. **Graded Lessons in Macramé, Knotting and Netting.** New York, Dover, 1971. 254p. illus. $2.00pa.

The original title was *Varied Occupations in String Work: Comprising Knotting, Netting, Looping, Plaiting, and Macramé*; it was first published in London in 1896. The Dover publication is an unaltered reprint of that work. It is a fascinating study of a newly revived aspect of Victorian handiwork. As the title indicates, the chapters are progressively graded, from beginner level to the more difficult. The drawings of knots and instructions are well done and the projects are not so dated as to be uninteresting. In fact, the major interest here will be for macramé beginners or enthusiasts who relish learning a little social history along with their craft.

376. **Woodstock Craftsman's Manual.** Ed. by Jean Young. New York, Praeger, 1972. 253p. illus. $10.00pa.

The subtitle continues: "a straight ahead guide to: weaving, pottery, macramé, beads, leather, tie-dye and batik, embroidery, silk screen, home recording, candles, crochet." An uneven and mostly amateur treatment of the above crafts. The section on resist dyeing is well done, with some information that even the experienced dyer might find interesting. The remaining topics of interest (such as weaving and macramé) are rather indifferently treated; the price of the paperback is not indifferent, however. The style is rather homey and cheery throughout. Illustrations consist of black and white diagrams and photographs.

RUG HOOKING

377. Beitler, Ethel Jane. **Hooked and Knotted Rugs.** New York, Sterling, 1973. 48p. illus. (Little Craft Series). $2.95.

The titles in Sterling's "Little Craft Series" appear to be uniformly well done; this one is no exception. The photographs of sources for ideas and rugs are excellent. The author shows how to hook a small rug, covering frames, transferring a design, and finishing, with information on several methods (knotting, latch hook, needle, and knotting). Although the book has everything the beginner needs to know, it will also interest those who are already involved in hooking, because the design ideas are extremely well done. Indexed.

378. Goodman, L. **Choice Hooked Rugs and the Original Frost's Hooked Rugs Patterns**. New York, American Life Foundation, 1972. 31p. illus. $2.95pa.

A reprint of the original Frost Company catalog of hooked rug stencils. The plates (all in blue and white) illustrating the rugs are from the originals used in their catalog printed in the 1800s. An interesting pamphlet in an historical sense. There are seven pages of introduction on design, materials, dyeing, and making the stencil. The introduction makes reference to knitted rugs and needlewoven rugs, but there are no details on these in the main body of the text. On inquiry, the reprint company answered that they did not have that section of the catalog so could not reprint it. Another disappointment is that the stencils for the patterns shown are not available, and the illustrations are not quite detailed enough to copy.

379. Kent, William Winthrop. **The Hooked Rug**. New York, Tudor, 1941; repr. Detroit, Mich., Tower Books, 1971. 210p. illus. $14.00.

A fine scholarly approach to the hooked rug as it has evolved through history, plus how-to-do-it information. Mr. Kent illustrates the historical aspects well, showing not only the rugs but the tools needed for them. He shows suitable materials for hooking and dyeing, and then goes into sources of design. A few chapters on searching for and collecting rugs are followed by sections on using, cleaning, and repairing rugs. Covers Europe and Great Britain as well as Canada and the United States. The book is not indexed.

380. Lawless, Dorothy. **Rug Hooking and Braiding for Pleasure and Profit**. New exp. ed. New York, T. Y. Crowell, 1962. 286p. illus. $5.95.

A well-known volume brought up to date with a supplement of 27 sections telling what is new in the field. Every single thing the beginner needs to know is here, clearly explained and illustrated. However, the author does not stop with that; she progresses through finishing, cleaning, pattern building (seven ways of doing rose leaves, for example) providing material that will inspire those who are already familiar with hooking and braiding. The chapter on how to market homemade rugs, although written before the new fabric identification laws, is of special interest, as is the one on how to teach rug hooking. Well indexed.

381. Meilach, Dona Z. **Making Contemporary Rugs and Wall Hangings**. New York, Abelard-Schuman, 1970. 159p. illus. $10.95.

No loom is required for the rugs discussed in this book. There are instructions for various techniques (hook, punch, rya, applique), with numerous photographs of finished rugs. The author discusses sources for designs, new materials, techniques, tools, care and cleaning, and exhibiting. No listing of contents, however, can indicate how excellent and thought-provoking are the hangings shown. The book will help the beginner, but will also serve as a source of inspiration for the more advanced.

382. Parker, Zenia Ley. **Hooked Rugs and Ryas**. Chicago, Regnery Publishing, 1973. 152p. illus. $6.95.

A low price for a book that is well conceived, well written, and well illustrated. If you want to learn how to make a rug, this is a good place to begin. The author approaches rugs with a no-nonsense attitude and a great deal of knowledge. Chapter seven is a "gallery of ideas" consisting of 40 pages of marvelous black and white photos, including a Museum of Modern Art rug by Arshile Gorky, Scandinavian ryas, and a simple tote bag, among others. There is a good section on supply sources, plus an index.

383. Roseaman, I. P. **Rugmaking, Knotted and Embroidered**. Leicester, England, Dryad Press. 36p. illus. $1.95pa.

Photographs of work in progress enliven this instructive book for beginners. Included among other techniques covered are knotting, needle-tufting, knitting, and embroidering. Rug design and edge finishing are discussed.

384. Scobey, Joan. **Rugmaking from Start to Finish**. New York, Lancer, 1973. 174p. illus. $1.95pa.

The characteristics and methods of four rug-making techniques are described: latch, punch, rya, and needlepoint. The author covers similarities and differences between the methods, and she also provides designs and ideas. The illustrations and diagrams are clear and to the point. There is a good section on sources for materials. Even though it lacks the excitement of Wiseman (entry 386), this book covers many techniques; and the price is right.

385. Stratton, Charlotte K. **Rug Hooking Made Easy**. New York, Harper and Row, 1955. 214p. illus. $6.95.

This work, which should interest both the novice and the experienced rug-maker, includes 149 black and white illustrations and eight color plates. The author shows her methods of shading colors and applies these techniques to motifs such as leaves, flowers, fruit, scrolls, and borders. There is also information on dyeing. A basic text for rug hooking.

386. Wiseman, Ann. **Rag Tapestries and Wool Mosaics.** New York, Van
 Nostrand Reinhold, 1969. 108p. illus. $7.95.

For all ages and all levels, this is one of the most exciting books ever written on rug hooking. If you are not interested now, you will be after reading this book. Precise text and numerous illustrations teach the beginner and inform the expert. All equipment needed is fully discussed, plus everything one must know in order to hook. A list of sources is also included. NBC-TV and the International Film Foundation in New York City have produced a documentary film (available through library/film co-ops) showing the author teaching at the Metropolitan Art Museum, New York. Twenty-five children created the rag tapestry *New York* under her guidance. A superb lesson in how to hook, create, and teach. See the film is possible, but by all means add the book to your collection. Another book by the author is *Rags, Rugs and Wool Pictures* (New York, Scribner's, 1968; $4.95), which is a charming book on rug hooking for children in grades 1 through 5. Ann Wiseman understands the art of rug hooking, but she also understands children.

387. Zarbock, Barbara J. **The Complete Book of Rug Hooking.** 2nd ed. New
 York, Van Nostrand Reinhold, 1969. 128p. illus. $7.95.

An excellent, complete introduction to rug hooking. The color and black and white photographs show many different kinds of designs, both traditional and modern. There is also a chapter on teaching rug hooking. While the beginner will benefit the most, this is a book that all will enjoy. History, present status, original designs, materials, equipment, techniques, color, dyeing, finishing, projects, and speed hooking are all well covered. The book contains a bibliography and supply source list. Indexed.

SELLING HANDICRAFTS

388. Clark, Leta W. **How to Make Money with Your Crafts.** New York,
 Morrow, 1973. 240p. $6.95.

Libraries and craftspersons will use this well-done and readable book to answer many questions. Good, sound advice abounds, plus an extensive appendix of information resources. It covers both retail and wholesale marketing, with details about expenses, operating procedures, taxes, etc.

A useful government publication that covers one aspect of the above book is "Starting and Managing a Swap Shop or Consignment Sale Shop"

(Washington, Superintendent of Documents, 1968; Starting and Managing Series, Vol. 15, 78p., $0.35). The reader should remember that the U.S. government is a gold-mine of information on setting up shop, selling, taxes, and other information.

389. Counts, Charles. **Encouraging American Craftsmen.** Washington, National Endowment for the Arts, 1972. 36p. illus. pa.

Single copies are available free from the National Endowment for the Arts. Multiple copies can be ordered from the Superintendent of Documents, Washington, D.C. ($0.45 ea.; Stock no. 3600-0010).

This pamphlet discusses handicrafts, prospects, problems, suggested solutions, recommendations, and recent progress. There is also information on setting up a craft shop or craft school, plus an excellent annotated bibliography. This is an essential pamphlet for anyone considering a venture into selling.

PERI☉DI☉ALS

Libraries, in particular, will want to look at craft magazines before ordering to see if the periodical in question fits their needs. Reviews are useful, but they cannot be the only criteria. For example, Bill Katz in *Magazines for Libraries*, 2nd ed. (New York, Bowker, 1972; p. 429), reviewed *Textile Crafts*; his view of it was entirely different from this bibliographer's view.

Local, state, and regional guilds of weavers often put out excellent newsletters, sometimes with sample swatches. These have not been listed. To find the local guild, either ask at a shop specializing in weaving equipment, ask a weaver, or write to the Handweavers Guild of America for the name and address of a guild in your area.

390. **American Fabrics.** Doris Publishing Company, 24 East 38th Street, New York, New York 10016. Quarterly. $24.00 per year.

This handsome production is one of the major journals in the field of fabrics. It has swatches, news from everywhere, and articles such as "Folk Prints of Japan" and "Batik."

391. **Artisan Crafts**. Star Route 4, Box M9-F, Reeds Spring, Missouri 65737. Quarterly. $5.00 per year.

A good down-to-earth magazine for the professional crafts person, not in any way a how-to-do-it. This is devoted to selling (how and where), helping craftspeople solve typical problems, alerting readers to pitfalls in craft shops, etc. There are also lists of supply sources and a directory listing service. A sample issue is $1.50.

392. **Australian Hand Weaver and Spinner: Quarterly Journal of the Hand Weavers' and Spinners' Guild of Australia**. Hand Weavers' and Spinners' Guild of Australia, Mrs. P. R. McMahon, Ed. 4 The Scarp, Castlecrag, N.S.W., 2068 Australia. Quarterly. $6.00 per year for overseas membership.

The contents fluctuate, since the journal is compiled by the Australian guilds on a rotating basis. It is a rather relaxed affair, with good information. On the whole, the "down under" weaver seems much more familiar with fleeces and spinning than the American weaver. The layout is a bit dull, but don't let it put you off an interesting journal.

393. **Craft/Midwest**. Box 42, Northbrook, Illinois 60062. Quarterly. $4.00 per year.

Ads, exhibit calendar, new products department, articles on craftsmen in many fields, and notices of shop openings and closings make this an interesting magazine. As the title indicates, its geographic area is the Midwest, but it will be useful to others—for example, those who want to exhibit, see exhibits, sell, or simply keep up on what's happening in one section of the country.

394. **Craft Horizons**. American Craftsmen's Council, 44 West 53rd Street, New York, New York 10019. Quarterly. $12.50 per year (see American Crafts Council under organizations).

Indexed in *Readers' Guide*. A beautifully produced magazine for all Craftsmen. It contains articles, a column called "craftsman's world," reviews of film and books, exhibitions, a calendar, and a list of places to show crafts. The review of shows (by state and city) is a major interest in each issue. The April issue each year has an excellent list of opportunities for "study and travel abroad." The list is a condensation of the ACC publication *ACC/ Directory of Craft Courses* (annual; $2.50 for members, $3.00 for non-members).

395. **The Craftsman's Gallery.** Box 645, Rockville, Maryland 20851. Quarterly. $8.00 per year (membership fee which includes, among other privileges, the Unicorn's book catalog and discount, Craftsman's Gallery and membership in the Guild of American Craftsmen).

The bulletin is largely made up of excellent black and white photographs of individual works (most of which are for sale), a few reports on people and things, book reviews, and miscellaneous items of interest to craftsmen.

396. **Design: The Magazine of Creative Art, for Teachers, Artists and Craftsmen.** Review Publishing Company, Inc., 1100 Waterway Blvd., Indianapolis, Indiana 46207. Bi-monthly. $7.00 per year. Indexed in *Readers' Guide.*

A useful magazine aimed at teachers of art and craft in elementary schools through colleges. It has art appreciation, instructions, announcements, and advertisements.

397. **Drafts and Designs.** Robin and Russ Handweavers, 533 North Adams Street, McMinnville, Oregon 97128. Monthly (except July and August). $5.00 per year.

A one-sheet flyer containing a swatch and giving complete thread, weaving, and finishing directions (and cost per yard) for four- to eight-harness weaves.

398. **Handweaver and Craftsman.** 220 Fifth Avenue, New York, New York 10001. Bi-monthly. $8.00 per year. Indexed in *Art Index.*

Not published since summer 1973. It contained information on techniques, new books, exhibits, yarns, tools, guilds, and much, much more. The advertisements alone were worth the issue price. In 1972 they published a yearbook, *Handweaver's Art* ($7.95), which described the progress of handweaving techniques, materials, tools and design in over 50 articles.

399. **Handweaver and Craftsman: Cumulated Index.** Available from Judith Arness, 3915 Washington Street, Kensington, Maryland 20795.

400. **The Looming Arts.** Mary Pendleton, Box 233, Jordan Road, Sedona, Arizona 86336. Bi-monthly. $4.50 per year (four-harness); $6.00 per year (with additional sample for multi-harness).

Looming Arts is a delightfully personal publication. It has a weaving editorial by Mary Pendleton, letters from weavers, activities at her studio, yarn sample selection, a four-harness sample with complete directions (the multi-harness issue has two samples—one for four-harness and one for more), articles by various well-known weavers, and a column on specific weaving problems.

401. **McCall's Needlework and Crafts.** McCall Pattern Co., 230 Park Avenue, New York, New York 10017. Semi-annual. $6.00 for two years (4 issues).

Lots of good color photos, fine projects, and a readers' exchange. All in all, a bargain for the home craftsperson. It usually covers knitting, crochet, needlepoint, quilting, little gifts, embroidery, crafts (batik, bread dough sculpture, macramé, rug making, weaving), and some projects especially for children. Contains patterns, a list of abbreviations, and helpful directions. Anyone at any level of creativity could use this. *Good Housekeeping* and *Ladies' Home Journal* publish similar magazines, though they don't have as many weaving and macramé projects as McCall's.

402. **The Master Weaver: Quarterly Bulletin for Handweavers.** Ed. by S. A. Zielinski. Z-Handicrafts, Fulford, Quebec, Canada. Quarterly. $5.50 per year ($1.50 for sample copy).

This quarterly, edited by a well-known weaver, deals with practical problems of handweaving on all levels. There are articles on designing, drafting, weaves, equipment, projects, yarns, exhibitions, and marketing.

403. **New Zealand Spinning Survey** (formerly **The Web**). The Handweavers Guild, Inc., P.O. Box 5873, Aukland, New Zealand. Volume 1, Number 1 was issued in August 1972, and is still available (as of June 1974) for $1.00 (New Zealand).

The magazine, prepared and published by the Aukland Handweavers Guild, carries articles on qualities of a good fleece, qualities of handspun, and other topics of interest. Staple length, crimp, appearance, preparation, spinning, and uses of finished wool are described for each breed of sheep covered. There are also comments on doing the fleece and an actual staple of the fleece. Thirteen samples are in Volume 1, Number 1. Very interesting to spinners. A subscription to *The Web*, the magazine of New Zealand's handweaving guild, is $3.80 (U.S.) a year—and well worth it.

404. **Ontario Handweavers and Spinners Quarterly Bulletin.** Order from Ms. Pauline Fanning, 207 Crescent Street, Peterborough, Ontario, Canada KGJ2G5. Quarterly. $5.00 per year; $5.25 U.S.

The *Bulletin* is prepared by the Guild and sent to all members. It contains news items about activities of interest to the members, plus articles about spinning, weaving, etc. Usually contains a woven swatch.

405. **Quarterly Journal of the Guilds of Weavers, Spinners and Dyers.** Win Evans, ed., China Court, Church Lane, Petham, Canterbury, Kent, England. Quarterly. $2.50 per year.

An interesting, serious journal from Great Britain. Its appearance is a trifle dull, but the articles are excellent. It includes reports from guilds around the country, interspersed with advertisements. There is also a classified section. The book reviews (signed by professionals such as Peter Collingwood) are critical and evaluative.

406. **The Shepherd: The Sheep Industry's Production and Management Paper.** Albert A. Lund, ed., Sheffield, Massachusetts 01257. Monthly. $4.00 per year.

The magazine for the sheep farmer. International in scope, it covers market trends, nutrition, etc.; while much of it is devoted to meat production, it is equally interested in wool production. Four back issues can be bought for only $1.50; this bargain allows the prospective subscriber to study the periodical before subscribing.

407. **Shuttle, Spindle and Dye-Pot.** 1013 Farmington Avenue, West Hartford, Connecticut 06107. Quarterly. $7.00 per year (available only to members of the Handweavers Guild of America).

This is the journal that all weavers, spinners, and dyers must take to keep abreast of their craft and most weavers would want to join their national organization anyway. Good articles with color illustrations, many regular columns, book reviews, a speakers' bureau, advertisements, and classified ads make the magazine well worth its cost. Some years have been indexed cumulatively; write to *Shuttle, Spindle and Dye-Pot* for the index.

408. **Textile Crafts.** Box 3216, Los Angeles, California 90028. Quarterly. $5.00 per year.

Articles on the textile crafts (e.g., weaving, lace making, dyeing) plus a calendar of events, short biographies of contributors, book reviews, and advertisements make up the issue. The illustrations are in black and white. A library would want to examine a sample copy before deciding, just to be sure it is what they want.

409. **Textile Museum Journal.** The Textile Museum, 2320 "S" Street N.W., Washington, D.C. 20008. Annual. $15.00 (includes Museum Newsletter and privileges of being a Museum member).

This production is not only sumptuous but necessary for textile scholars, libraries, and all those interested in rugs and fabrics. The *Journal* includes scholarly articles, bibliographies, and book reviews; the *Newsletter* carries news of the museum, its activities, and the staff.

410. **Threads in Action.** Virginia Harvey, ed. Available now through HTH Publishers. Quarterly. $2.50 each issue. Published from Volume 1, No. 1 (September 1969) through Volume 5, No. 1 (1974).

A periodical covering primarily macramé, by a well-known craftsperson. It included sample threads, photographs, diagrams, a personal column, and a glossary with knot instructions. It was good, as one would expect from a Virginia Harvey publication. No longer published.

411. **Warp and Weft.** Robin and Russ Handweavers, 533 North Adams Street, McMinnville, Oregon 97128. Monthly (except July and August). $4.50 per year.

Each issue contains one swatch for a four-harness loom, with complete directions for weaving (including price per yard). Also includes an editorial chat from Russ, a few advertisements, and book reviews. Swatch-type periodicals are particularly valuable for beginning weavers.

412. **The Web** (New Zealand). See **Spinning Survey**.

413. **Webe Mit: Zeitschrift für das Handweben.** Webe-Mit Verlag, 7065 Manolzweiler Post Winterbach, W. Germany. Quarterly. $5.00 per year.

This German handweaving magazine will be useful for some. It is illustrated and carries weaving projects and articles.

414. **Black Sheep Newsletter.** Sachiye Jones, Route 2, Box 123-D, Monroe, Oregon. Quarterly. Single issue $0.35; $1.00 per year.

Begun in 1973, this mimeographed newsletter shows all the signs of being a healthy publication. The spinner will find that the information in it is unique, personal, and well worth the dollar. The many contributors comment on such subjects as buying fleeces, raising black sheep, testing tensile strength, etc. There is a directory of black sheep farmers, and there are advertisements.

DIRECTORY OF
ORGANIZATIONS
AND
SUPPLY SOURCES

ORGANIZATIONS

Joining with others of like interest will help the craftsperson keep abreast, change, receive stimulation, meet new people, and know current fashion ideas, whether good, bad, or indifferent. Membership in local and national organizations can be most rewarding and a great deal of fun.

Although only national organizations have been listed in this book, there are many excellent local, state, and regional guilds. The Handweavers Guild of America will furnish a contact name for your locality upon request.

American Crafts Council, 44 West 53rd Street, New York, New York 10019.

Founded in 1943 to stimulate interest in and appreciation of the work of American craftsmen, the council has been effective and is carrying on vital programs. Craftsman/Sustaining Members ($18.50 for individuals; $22.00 joint) receive six issues of *Craft Horizons*, six issues of *Outlook* (the Council's newsletter), plus reduced rates for all other ACC publications, slide rentals, film purchases, and Council-sponsored events; a vote in regional and national Council elections; free admission to the Museum of Contemporary Crafts; invitations to its exhibition previews; complimentary brochures describing exhibitions in the Little and 2nd Floor Galleries; and the ACC Annual Report. Participating Members ($35.00) receive the above benefits plus complimentary copies of the Museum of Contemporary Crafts catalogs. Sponsoring Members ($100.00) will receive, in addition to the above benefits, free registration at Council-sponsored events and complimentary copies of ACC publications. Subscribing Members ($12.50) receive *Craft Horizons* and free admission to the Museum of Contemporary Crafts. See entry 394 for a review of *Craft Horizons.*

Among the other publications of the American Crafts Council are its exhibit catalogs. The ones that are of most interest here are: *Sculpture in Fiber, 1972* (16p., 18 color plates; $2.00 for members, $2.50 for non-members), which includes pictures of three-dimensional non-woven fiber constructions and biographical information about the artists; and *Dorothy Liebes, 1970* (36p., 24 color plates; $2.00 for members, $2.25 for non-members), which contains photographs of textiles by the late Dorothy Liebes, an American weaver and designer.

The ACC also issues a biennial, nationwide directory of outlets for selling crafts ($3.00 to members, and $3.95 to non-members).

Guild of American Craftsmen, Box 645, Rockville, Maryland 20851.

A new organization from the Unicorn Bookshop. Membership ($8.00) gives one a subscription to the *Craftsman's Gallery*, a copy of the Unicorn's catalog, *Books for Craftsmen*, a 10 percent discount on items purchased from the Unicorn, and other benefits. The Guild's aim is to promote an appreciation of the crafts and to help craftsmen find a market for their goods.

Handweavers Guild of America, 1013 Farmington Avenue, West Hartford, Connecticut 06107.

The main handweavers' guild in the United States publishes *Shuttle, Spindle and Dye-Pot*, which is included in the membership fee of $7.00 a year. The Handweavers Guild of America underwrites scholarships, Convergence (a biannual meeting of handweavers, spinners, and other craftsmen from around the world), and generally anything of interest to these particular craftspeople. Continuing support of the H.G.A. and its programs is a must for weavers, spinners and dyers, but it is also a pleasure.

Handweaving guilds, local and regional.

Handweavers will want to explore their area's local and regional guilds to see which has a program that fits their particular needs. Some guilds are social, some have workshops, some programs—their emphases vary widely.

Textile Museum, 2320 "S" Street, N.W., Washington, D.C. 20008.
$15.00 per year for individual; $25.00 per year for family
membership.

This is *the* museum in the United States dedicated to textiles. Membership includes the handsome magazine, the museum newsletter, and privileges
of the museum, among other benefits. Certainly every dedicated textile
scholar will want to support this fine organization.

SUPPLY SOURCES

The source list is selective, with no claim to being complete. Its purpose
is to serve as a starting point. The best place to locate sources is in the adver-
tisement and classified sections of periodicals such as *Shuttle, Spindle and
Dye-Pot.*

Craft and Hobby Book Service, P.O. Box 626, Pacific Grove, California
93950.

Used to specialize in weaving and other craft books and magazines; now
combined with Unicorn. See Unicorn for address.

Craftool: Tools, Equipment and Books for the Creative Crafts. Yearly
catalog. Craftool Company, 1421 West 240 Street, Harbor City,
California 90710.

Lists batik, weaving, and other books, some of which are Craftool
products; others are the usual craft books, such as those published by Dryad
Press.

K. R. Drummond, Bookseller, Hart Grove, Ealing Common, London W5,
England.

Specializes in books and magazines on weaving, spinning and dyeing,
plus rare items. Excellent source. By appointment only.

Horizon Handicrafts Book Service, 220 Fifth Avenue, New York, New
York 10001.

Handweaver and Craftsman magazine has put together a book club for
craftsmen through Horizon Handicrafts. The $5.00 membership fee entitles
the club member to a 15 percent discount on all books offered. The club
catalog, listing all books offered, is free and anyone can buy from it at list

price. Many crafts are covered: canework, reed and raffia, spinning, dyeing, handweaving, batik, tie-dye, macramé and knots, knitting, crochet, collage, decoupage, rubbings, leather, and more. An interesting question is whether or not it can stay in operation without *Handweaver and Craftsman*?

Museum Books, Inc., 48 East 43rd Street, New York, New York 10017.

Specializes in craft books of all sorts. They will send a catalog of titles available.

Robin and Russ Handweavers, 533 North Adams Street, McMinnville, Oregon 97128.

Specializes in books on weaving, spinning, dyeing, macramé, bobbin lace, sprang, and related fields.

School Products Company, Inc., 312 East 23rd Street, New York, New York 10010.

Books and equipment for weaving and spinning.

Straw into Gold, 5509 College, Oakland, California 94618.

An excellent source for spinning and dyeing supplies including dye plant seeds.

The Unicorn: Books for Craftsmen, Box 645, Rockville, Maryland 20851.

A rather complete selection of books for the craftsman in all the areas covered in this bibliography. Their annotated catalog of holdings is available for $0.50.

DIRECTORY OF PUBLISHERS

(Individuals publishing their own works
have been entered under their last name.)

Abelard-Schuman, Ltd.
257 Park Avenue South
New York, New York 10010

Agricultural Extension Service
General Extension Division
University of Minnesota
Minneapolis, Minnesota 55455

Allman and Sons, Ltd.
17-19 Foley Street
London W1A 1DR, England

American Life Foundation Study
   Institute
P.O. Watkins Glen
New York, New York 14891

American Rabbit Journal
Carmel, Indiana 46032

Arco Publishing Co., Inc.
219 Park Avenue South
New York, New York 10003

Art Vivant, Inc.
173 Highbridge Road
New Rochelle, New York 10804

Ballantine Books, Inc.
101 Fifth Avenue
New York, New York 10003

Bankfield Museum (see Museums
Publishing)

Bare Cove Weavers
Box 183
Hingham, Massachusetts 02043

A. S. Barnes and Co.
Forsgate Drive
Cranbury, New Jersey 08512

Belmont Productions, Inc.
185 Madison Avenue
New York, New York 10016

Charles A. Bennett Co., Inc.
809 West Detweiller Drive
Peoria, Illinois 61614

Best-West Publications
Box 759
Palm Desert, California 92260

G. Bill and Sons, Ltd.
York House
Portugal Street
London WC2, England

Bishop Museum Press
P.O. Box 6037
Honolulu, Hawaii 96818

Grace D. Blum
440 Crestview Road
Southern Pines, North Carolina 28387

Bonanza Books (see Crown
Publishers)

Book Barn
P.O. Box 245
Storrs, Connecticut 06268

Bramhall House
Division of Crown Publishers
419 Park Avenue South
New York, New York 10016

Branden Press
221 Columbus Avenue
Boston, Massachusetts 02116

Charles T. Branford Co.
28 Union Street
Newton Centre, Massachusetts 02159

British Museum
The Trustee of the British Museum
6 Bedford Square
London WC 1B 3RA, England

British Wool Marketing Board
Kew Bridge House
Kew Bridge Road
Isleworth
Middlesex, England

or

British Wool Marketing Board
Wool House
Carlton Gardens
London SW1, England

Brooklyn Botanic Garden
1000 Washington Avenue
Brooklyn, New York 11225

Brooklyn Museum
Eastern Parkway
Brooklyn, New York 11238

William C. Brown and Co.
135 South Locust Street
Dubuque, Iowa 52003

Bruce Publishing Company
2642 University Avenue
St. Paul, Minnesota 55114

Carnegie Institution of Washington
1530 "P" Street, N.W.
Washington, D.C. 20005

M. L. and W. E. Channing
35 Main Street
Marion, Massachusetts 02738

Chilton Book Company
401 Walnut Street
Philadelphia, Pennsylvania 19106

Collier-Macmillan (see Crowell
Collier and Macmillan, Inc.)

William Collins and Sons, Ltd.
215 Park Avenue South
New York, New York 10003

Bonny Cook
Route 7, Box 7843
Bainbridge Island, Washington
98110

Cornell Maritime Press, Inc.
Box 109
Cambridge, Maryland 21613

Cowles Book Co., Inc. (see Henry
Regnery Co.)

Craft and Hobby Book Service
P.O. Box 626
Pacific Grove, California 93950
(Now send inquiries to The Unicorn.)

Craft Course Publishers
Rosemead, California 91770

Craft/Midwest Magazine
Box 42
Northbrook, Illinois 60062

Thomas Y. Crowell Co.
201 Park Avenue South
New York, New York 10003

Crowell Collier and Macmillan, Inc.
866 Third Avenue
New York, New York 10022

Crown Publishers, Inc.
419 Park Avenue South
New York, New York 10016

CUM Textiles Industries, Ltd.
Roemersgade 5
1362 Copenhagen K. Denmark
(See any recent issue of *Shuttle,
Spindle and Dye-Pot* for a list of
CUM dealers in the United States.)

Mary F. Davidson
Route 1
Gatlinburg, Tennessee 37738

Davis Publications, Inc.
50 Portland Street
Worchester, Massachusetts 01608

Marguerite P. Davison
Box 263
Swathmore, Pennsylvania 19081

John DeGraff, Inc.
34 Oak Avenue
Tuckahoe, New York 10707

Denver Art Museum
100 West 14th Avenue Parkway
Denver, Colorado 80204

Denver Museum of Natural History
City Park
Denver, Colorado 80205

Department of Education
Marlborough Street 1
Dublin, Ireland

Doubleday and Co., Inc.
277 Park Avenue
New York, New York 10017
and
Garden City, New York 11530

Dover Publications, Inc.
180 Varick Street
New York, New York 10014

Drake Publishers, Ltd.
381 Park Avenue South
New York, New York 10016

Dryad Press
Northgates
Leicester LE1 4QR, England

East River Publishers (Request
through suppliers who handle
craft books.)

Edita S. A. Lausanne
7, Rue de Genève
Lausanne, Switzerland

Les Editions de Bonvent S.A.
136, route de Chêne
CH-1224 Genève/Chêne-Bougeries
Switzerland

Emerson Books, Inc.
251 West 19th Street
New York, New York 10011

Josephine Estes
524 Watertown Street
Newton, Massachusetts 02158

Fairchild Publications, Inc.
7 East 12th Street
New York, New York 10003

Finch Press Reprints
337 East Huron Street
Ann Arbor, Michigan 48108

Fine Arts Press
Santa Ana, California

Flax Spinners and Manufacturers
Association
1 Bank Street
Dundee, Scotland

Förlag [sic]
Luntmakargatan 13, Sweden

Funk and Wagnalls, Inc.
53 East 77th Street
New York, New York 10021

GPO (See Superintendent of
Documents.)

Gale Research Co.
Book Tower
Detroit, Michigan 48226

Golden Press
850 Third Avenue
New York, New York 10022

Gordon's Naturals
P.O. Box 506
Roseburg, Oregon 97470

Government Printing Office (See
Superintendent of Documents.)

Grosset and Dunlap, Inc.
51 Madison Avenue
New York, New York 10010

Gryphon Books
Division of Gale Research Co.
(See Gale Research Co.)

HGA (See Handweavers Guild of
America.)

HTH Publishers
1607-A East Edinger
Santa Ana, California 92705

Hacker Art Books, Inc.
54 West 57th Street
New York, New York 10019

Paul Hamlyn
Hamlyn House
The Centre
Feltham, Middlesex,
England

Handweavers
305 State Street
Los Altos, California 94022

Handweavers Guild of America, Inc.
1013 Farmington Avenue
West Hartford, Connecticut 06107

Harper and Row, Publishers
49 East 33rd Street
New York, New York 10016

Ruth Ketterer Harris
1134 Merrill Springs Road
Madison, Wisconsin 53705

Heard Museum
22 East Monte Vista Road
Phoenix, Arizona 85004

Hearthside Press, Inc.
445 Northern Blvd.
Great Neck, New York 11021

Her Majesty's Stationary Office
49 High Holborn
London WC 1, England

P. C. Herwig Co.
264 Clinton Street
Brooklyn, New York 11201

Holt, Rinehart and Winston
383 Madison Avenue
New York, New York 10017

Iowa State University Press
Press Building
Ames, Iowa 50012

Kircher
355 Marburg/L
Postfach 1408
West Germany

Kustannusosakeyhtiö Otava
Uudenmannkatu 10
SF-00120
Helsinki, Finland

Lancer Books, Inc.
1560 Broadway
New York, New York 10036

Lane Magazine and Book Co.
Menlo Park, California 94025

Leclerc (see Nilus Leclerc.)

LeJeune
Sunnyvale, California 94086

Lerner Publications Co.
241 First Avenue North
Minneapolis, Minnesota 55401

Lily Mills Company
Shelby, North Carolina 28150

J. B. Lippincott Co.
East Washington Square
Philadelphia, Pennsylvania 19105

Longmans, Green and Co., Ltd.
48 Grosvenor Street
London W 1, England

Loom Books
318 Pacheo Street
Santa Cruz, California 95060

The Loom Room
M. E. Freeborn
R.D. 1
New Hope, Pennsylvania 18938

M.I.T. Press
28 Carleton Street
Cambridge, Massachusetts 02142

McCall Publishing Co.
230 Park Avenue
New York, New York 10017

McGraw Hill Book Co.
330 West 42nd Street
New York, New York 10020

The Macmillan Co. (See Crowell
Collier and Macmillan, Inc.)

Manual Arts Press (See Charles A.
Bennett Co., Inc.)

Mendocino County Historical Society
603 West Perkins Street
Ukiah, California 95482

Michigan Graphic Corporation
8777 Main
Whitmore Lake, Michigan 48189

Mills and Boon Ltd.
17-19 Foley Street
London W1A 1DR, England

William Morrow and Co.
105 Madison Avenue
New York, New York 10016
(Send orders to: 6 Henderson Drive,
West Caldwell, New Jersey 07006

Mrs. Carl F. Murray
713 Quaker Drive
Friendswood, Texas 77546

Museum für Volkerkunde
Basel, Switzerland

Museum of Navajo Ceremonial Art
P.O. Box 5153
Santa Fe, New Mexico 87501

Museum of New Mexico Press
P.O. Box 2087
Santa Fe, New Mexico 87501

Museum of Northern Arizona
Box 1389
Flagstaff, Arizona 86001

Museums Publishing
Bankfield Museum
Halifax, England

National Association of Scottish
  Woolen Manufacturers
27 Charlotte Square
Edinburgh, Scotland

National Endowment for the Arts
Washington, D.C. 20506

New York Graphic Society, Ltd.
140 Greenwich Avenue
Greenwich, Connecticut 06830

Margaret Newman
1001 East David Road
Clearwater, Florida 33516

Nilus Leclerc
L'Isletville
Quebec, Canada

Normaway Handcrafts
Sydney, Cape Breton Island,
Nova Scotia

Northland Press
P.O. Box N
Flagstaff, Arizona 86001

Octopus Books
59 Grosvenor Street
London W 1, England

Oregon Educational and Public
  Broadcasting Service
Oregon State University
Corvallis, Oregon 97331

Oxford University Press, Inc.
200 Madison Avenue
New York, New York 10016

Pantheon Books, Inc.
201 East 50th Street
New York, New York 10022

Las Pajaritas Studio
6901 Guadalupe Trail N.W.
Albuquerque, New Mexico 87108

Hazel Pearson Handicrafts
Rosemead, California 91776

Penland School of Crafts
Penland, North Carolina 28765

Praeger Publishers, Inc.
111 Fourth Avenue
New York, New York 10003

Prentice-Hall, Inc.
Englewood Cliffs, New Jersey
  07632

RIT Consumer Service Department
Best Foods Division
CPC International Inc.
Indianapolis, Indiana 46206

A. H. and A. W. Reed Ltd.
182 Wakefield Street
Wellington, New Zealand

Henry Regnery Co.
114 West Illinois Street
Chicago, Illinois 60610

Reinhold Book Corporation
430 Park Avenue
New York, New York 10022

Rio Grande Press, Inc.
La Casa Escuele
Glorieta, New Mexico 87535

Robin and Russ Handweavers
533 North Adams Street
McMinnville, Oregon 97128

Roy Publishers, Inc.
30 East 74th Street
New York, New York 10021

Royal Ontario Museum
Toronto, Canada

Ryerson Press (See McGraw-Hill.)

Sagadohoc Press
Box 448
Georgetown, Maine 04548

Salish Weavers
Box 307
Chilliwack, B.C., Canada

Schocken Books, Inc.
67 Park Avenue
New York, New York 10016

Charles Scribner's Sons
597 Fifth Avenue
New York, New York 10017

E. A. Seemann Publishing, Inc.
14701 S.W. 84th Court
Miami, Florida 33158

Select Books
P.O. Box 626
Pacific Grove, California 93950

Serenity Weavers
111 West 7th
Eugene, Oregon 97401

Seven Valleys Weavers Guild
1906 Preble Road
Preble, New York 13141

Shorey Book Store
815 Third Avenue
Seattle, Washington 98104

Shuttlecraft Guild (Most of its publications have been reprinted by HTH--see entry.)

Paula Simmons
Suquamish, Washington 98392

Simon and Schuster, Inc.
630 Fifth Avenue
New York, New York 10020

Smithsonian Institution Press
Editorial and Publications Division
Washington, D.C. 20560

Marion Burr Sober
Box 294-3
Plymouth, Michigan 48170

Betty Soderburg
2577 Beachwood Drive
Hollywood, California 90028

Some Place
2990 Adeline Street
Berkeley, California 94703

South Ontario Unit of the Herb
  Society of America
Order publications from
Mrs. Dorothy Kirk
R.R. 2, Owen Sound
Ontario N4K 5NA, Canada

Spincraft
Box 332
Richardson, Texas 75080

Stein and Day Publishers
7 East 48th Street
New York, New York 10017

Sterling Publishing Co., Inc.
419 Park Avenue South
New York, New York 10016

Straw into Gold
5509 College Avenue
P.O. Box 2904
Oakland, California 94618

Studio Vista, Ltd.
Blue Star House
Highgate Hill
London N19, England

Sunset Books (See Lane Magazine
  and Book Co.)

Suntone Press
P.O. Box 2321
Santa Fe, New Mexico 87501

Superintendent of Documents
U.S. Government Printing Office
Washington, D.C. 20402

Taplinger Publishing Co., Inc.
200 Park Avenue South
New York, New York 10003

Textile Book Service
266 Lake Avenue
P.O. Box 178
Metuchen, New Jersey 08840

Textile Museum
2320 "S" Street N.W.
Washington, D.C. 20008

Threshold
443 Sebastopol Avenue
Santa Rosa, California 95401

Thys'lldo
Ken and Dularla Chapin
2178 Pompey Fabius Road
R.D. 1
Fabius, New York 13063

Osma Gallinger Tod Studio
319 Mendoza Avenue
Coral Gables, Florida 33306

Tudor Publishing Co.
572 Fifth Avenue
New York, New York 10036

Charles E. Tuttle Co.
28 South Main Street
Rutland, Vermont 05701

The Unicorn
Box 645
Rockville, Maryland 20851

United States Government, all
  departments (See Superintendent
  of Documents.)

University of California Press
2223 Fulton Street
Berkeley, California 94720

University of Oklahoma Press
1005 Asp Avenue
Norman, Oklahoma 73069

University of Texas Press
P.O. Box 7819
University Station
Austin, Texas 78712

University of Toronto Press
Campus St. George
Toronto 181, Canada

or

33 East Tupper Street
Buffalo, New York 14208

University of Washington Press
Seattle, Washington 98105

Van Nostrand Reinhold Co.
450 West 33rd Street
New York, New York 10001

Viking Press, Inc.
625 Madison Avenue
New York, New York 10022

Watson-Guptill Publications, Inc.
165 West 46th Street
New York, New York 10036

Franklin Watts, Inc.
845 Third Avenue
New York, New York 10022

Wehman Bros.
158 Main Street
Hackensack, New Jersey 07601

Wesleyan University Press
100 Riverview Center
Middletown, Connecticut 06457

Western Publishing Co., Inc.
1220 Mound Avenue
Racine, Wisconsin 53404

Wezäta Förlag A.B.
P.O. Box 5057
Grafiska Vägen
S-40222 Göteborg, Sweden

Wheelwright Press
975 South West Temple
Salt Lake City, Utah 84101

Margaret Windeknecht
1298 Talcot Place
Decatur, Georgia 30033

Wool Education Center
200 Clayton Street
Denver, Colorado 80206

Allan Wyngate
London (See source list—order
through a craft book jobber.)

INDEX

References are to entry numbers for authors and titles, and to page numbers for organizations and works mentioned in the annotations for organizations. Works are also indexed by broad subject.